712.6
K179s

JAN 2006

CH

Serene Gardens

Amidst the splendor of the scene,

and the silence,

I was filled with a wonderful peace.

Basho

Yoko Kawaguchi

Serene Gardens

creating Japanese design and detail

in the western garden

Trafalgar Square Publishing

For Kiyoshi and Junko Kawaguchi, and Simon Rees.

Contents

Introduction 7

Chapter one
Traditional Japanese Gardens 18
Historical context, design, choice of plants

• The hill and pond garden 20 • The dry garden 34 • The tea garden 44 • The courtyard garden 54

Chapter two
The Elements of a Japanese Garden 64
How to choose, lay out and care for the components of a Japanese garden

• Plants 66 • Rocks 76 • Water 84 • Sand 96 • Paths and stepping-stones 98 • Bridges 104
• Stone lanterns 110 • Pergolas 112 • Fences 114 • Borrowed vistas 120

Chapter three
Plant Directory 122

• Trees 124 • Shrubs 128 • Berries 130 • Ground-cover 130 • Grasses and bamboos 132 • Mosses 132
• Ferns 132 • Tropical specimen plants 134 • Foliage and flowers 134 • Aquatic plants 134 • Non-traditional alternatives 136

Resources

• Hardiness zones 138 • Bibliography 140
• Gardens to visit 140
• Photography credits and acknowledgements 141
• General index 142 • Plant index 143

Introduction

All over the world people are attracted to Japanese gardens, usually because they provide a tranquil environment, designed to give the impression of a natural landscape at its most serene. They possess a unique aura of calm, which derives from an economical, almost minimal use of materials, whether for building or planting.

A garden in the Japanese style is intended to offer peace and quiet contemplation, with restraint, order, harmony and decorum as the guiding design principles. It is an expression of love for living things, acceptance of the transience of Nature reflected in the changing seasons, and an inspired vision of the eternal.

From the tiniest courtyards to the grandest parks, Japanese gardens invite one to linger and savor their timeless quality.

Japanese-style gardens first became popular in the West in the second half of the nineteenth century. They were part of a craze for all things Japanese which swept Europe and America for about fifty years after the country first became more accessible. Until then, Japan had kept her doors tightly shut against the rest of the world with a brief exception in the seventeenth century, after which only a small group of Chinese and Dutch merchants, confined to a tiny island outside Nagasaki, were allowed to continue trading. The Dutch East India Company sent back to Europe Japanese porcelain and lacquered (japanned) chests and cabinets. What most people knew of Japan were the flowers, birds, pine-trees and islands painted on these household objects.

At first, it was the idea of Chinese rather than Japanese gardens that captured the imagination of Europeans, following the well-established fashion for Chinese motifs on porcelain, furniture and fabrics. When the first western accounts of real Chinese gardens began to appear in the second quarter of the eighteenth century, they sparked off a vogue for mock-Chinese garden houses, which began in Britain and quickly spread to France and other countries. Pavilions and pagodas were used instead of classical temples, by then an established feature of English landscape gardens. In the western imagination, Chinese gardens were idyllic pleasure-grounds where languid ladies and gentlemen spent their time amusing themselves, drinking wine and playing musical instruments. When travellers returning from the Far East described real Chinese gardens as lacking the symmetry of European ones of the time (most of Europe was still under the influence of the French formal style), this apparent lack of constraint was welcomed by those eager to throw off the chains of French tradition. The charm of the Chinese style was thought to lie in the variety of scenery contained in one garden. Sir William Chambers (1723–96), the designer of the Chinese Pagoda and other buildings in Kew Gardens, felt that Lancelot "Capability" Brown (1715–83), the great eighteenth-century English landscape gardener, was going too far towards a "natural" style of open landscape. In his *Dissertation on Oriental Gardening* (1772), Chambers proposed a greater use of contours, a more informal and varied style of planting shrubs, especially flowering ones, and the use of buildings to add diversity to the landscape. His theories were presented as though they were the tastes of the Chinese.

Japanese gardens were also seen through a haze of preconceptions about the luxuriant, sensual East. They were considered to be as highly artificial as Chinese ones, but while Chambers believed that a careful use of artifice enhanced a garden, Japanese gardens were often described as mannered and affected. In other fields of art, Japanese styles did not produce such doubtful reactions. Once Japan began to open her doors, more screens, fans, silks and wood-block prints than ever were exported to the West, with an immediate effect on artists and

right: *A cascade can be glimpsed between drifts of spring color, here camellias and flowering cherries. The neatly pruned hedge in the front emphasizes the clean, elegant form and the height of the cherry tree.*

Keep other trees with long trunks, such as the crape myrtle (Lagerstroemia indica), *Stewartia pseudocamellia, and species azaleas such as* Rhododendron reticulatum *and* R. quinquefolium *similarly uncluttered with underplanting. They will then provide a valuable focal point in the garden.*

other people. While painters experimented with unfamiliar Japanese techniques, shops started catering to the taste of the British and French for exotic *objets d'art*. In 1875, Arthur Lasenby Liberty launched his first shop in London selling Japanese silks. Operas and operettas on Japanese themes were soon appearing on the stage in London and Paris, among them Camille Saint-Saëns' *La Princesse jaune* (1872) and Gilbert and Sullivan's *The Mikado* (1885). Both of these made Japan a land of fantasy, though Gilbert actually visited a Japanese village at an exhibition in Knightsbridge about the time *The Mikado* went into rehearsal. This village employed craftsmen, dancers, musicians and acrobats brought over from Japan; there was also a tea-house and a garden with serving maidens whom Gilbert photographed.

Images of Japan

The theatre had a growing pool of sources to draw on. Many travel books were published between 1870 and 1890, recording the experiences of the first intrepid visitors. Novels soon followed, often romantic tales about Japanese women and western men, set in a decadent, sensual Japan. Pierre Loti's *Madame Chrysanthème* (1888), based on his experiences as a naval officer in Nagasaki, was made into an opera by André Messager in 1893, and both forms had some influence on Giacomo Puccini when he came to compose *Madame Butterfly* (1904). Loti's central character arrives in Japan expecting to see tiny paper houses surrounded by flowers and green gardens. Though he thinks nothing of this culture, he looks forward to seeing his ideas of Japan realized, but after some time there his prejudices turn into a deep dislike for what he interprets as Japanese artificiality. Loti's novel helped to spread the image of miniature gardens with misshapen pine-trees, diminutive bridges and minute waterfalls — a landscape inhabited by flitting, child-like women

with butterfly sleeves, glimpsed beneath the curving eaves of a tea-house.

Another popular western image of Japan was of a land smothered in flowers. At the end of the nineteenth century, one of the greatest hits on the London stage was a musical extravaganza called *The Geisha*, which opened at Daly's Theatre in 1896. The curtains opened on a view of the Tea-house of Ten Thousand Joys, with geishas posing on a humpbacked red bridge spanning a carp-pond. Flowers were used to establish the "Japanese" setting: in the first act, wisteria dripped from the eaves of the tea-house (though wisteria is never grown against a house in Japan); in the second, the stage was overflowing with chrysanthemums, which flower much later (though no time was supposed to have passed between the acts). Japanese gardens were associated with a heady mixture of flowers and nubile young women. In the last act of *Madame Butterfly*, the heroine and her maid, Suzuki, dance around their house, scattering cherry-blossoms, peach-blossoms, violets, jasmine, roses, lilies, verbena and tuberoses to welcome Butterfly's American husband, Pinkerton.

Meanwhile, richer gardeners made it fashionable to create Japanese gardens in a corner of their estates. Japanese plants, including maples, sago palms and double-flowered kerria, had been brought to Europe late in the eighteenth century by Carl Pehr Thunberg (1743–1828), a Swedish doctor and naturalist who had travelled to Japan with the Dutch. Many more plants, among them the single-flowered kerria, many azaleas, Japanese rush (*Acorus gramineus*), the plantain lily (*Hosta plantaginea*) and the spotted laurel (*Aucuba japonica*) were introduced to Europe by Philipp Franz von Siebold (1796–1866), a German physician and naturalist who also spent some time at the Dutch East India Company trading station at Nagasaki. Both Thunberg and Siebold wrote books about Japanese plants, and both described their travels in

the country. From the time of Japan's opening to the West until the outbreak of the First World War, many more plant collectors went to Japan, among them Robert Fortune (1813–80), James Gould Veitch (1839–70) and E. H. Wilson (1876–1930) from Britain, Carl Johann Maximowicz (1827–91) from Russia and David Fairchild (1869–1954) from the United States. Fairchild is remembered in particular for his passion for flowering cherries; thanks to his enthusiasm, Japanese cherries were planted along the Potomac River in Washington, DC. In turn, Fairchild sent saplings of American flowering dogwoods to Tokyo, and these trees are still immensely popular in Japan today.

Diplomats coming home were among the first to make Japanese gardens in Britain. A. B. Freeman-Mitford (1837–1916), who became Baron Redesdale in 1902 (and was the grandfather of the writer Nancy Mitford), was one of them. After publishing *Tales of Old Japan* (1871), he planted fifty species and varieties of hardy bamboo in his garden at Batsford Park, in Gloucestershire. His book *The Bamboo Garden* (1896) described the collection. At the turn of the century, Louis Greville (1856–1941) built a Japanese-style garden at Heale House, Wiltshire; it included a thatched tea-house and a vermilion bridge. By this time Josiah Conder's books on Japanese gardening had also appeared. An architect commissioned to design western buildings in Japan, Conder (1852–1920) wrote two studies of gardening traditions there: *The Flowers of Japan and the Art of Floral Arrangement* (1891) and *Landscape Gardening in Japan* (1893). In these books, especially the latter, readers found more bridges, stone lanterns, rocks and cropped pines to copy.

It had been known for almost a hundred years that the Chinese practised bonsai, the art of growing dwarf trees in shallow pots. An exhibit of bonsai trees was put on show in Liverpool in 1872 in honor

left: *Contrasting autumn colors at Batsford Park in Gloucestershire. The umbrella-shaped Prunus hillieri "Spire" (rear right) forms a canopy over the gazebo, while the more informally shaped Acer rubrum helps to blend this group into the woodland background. The vibrantly colored Acer palmatum "Osakazuki" reflects the shape of the prunus, giving the group its coherence.*

below: *Japanese pines and maples are some of the most popular choices for bonsai as well as being the most important trees used in the Japanese garden.*

The idea of garden topiary is essentially the same as that of bonsai, to refine the shape of the tree to bring out its hidden beauty. The maple in this picture belongs to the var. heptalobum *group, having the classical seven-lobed leaf form.*

of the Japanese Ambassador and his colleagues. In the first two decades of the twentieth century, the fashion for Japanese gardening, both large-scale and in miniature, reached its peak. There was a steady trade in bonsai trees, and gardeners were brought

from Japan to build gardens for wealthy patrons as Japanese gardens became the rage among the English Edwardian upper classes. The best surviving examples from the period include Tatton Park in Cheshire; Cottered, near Buntingford,

Hertfordshire; and Tully, near Kildare (where another part of the estate is now the home of the Irish National Stud). Mount Ephraim, near Faversham in Kent, has a Japanese rock garden set in a hillside. Coombe Wood, near Kingston, Surrey, is on the site of James Veitch's own nursery, which sold plants originally collected by Veitch himself, his son James Gould, and E. H. Wilson. The garden here still contains many of Veitch's plantings, and it has taken in the Japanese-style garden built on the estate next door, which has a particularly beautiful water garden. Iford Manor, near Bradford-on-Avon, Wiltshire, is the former home of the architect and landscape gardener Harold Peto (1854–1933), who designed the grounds of Heale House. Iford, too, had a Japanese garden, now being restored. Of the various elements of Japanese gardens imitated in Europe, it was probably the use of water that was most easily appreciated. Ponds in naturalistic settings play an important part in the gardens created by painters as different as the Impressionist Claude Monet (1840–1926) and E. A. Hornel (1864–1933), one of the group of artists who were known as "The Glasgow Boys".

Landscape in miniature

The concepts underlying the Japanese art of arranging groups of rocks in the garden have perhaps been less easy to approach for western gardeners, but as an interest in eastern religions has burgeoned in the last thirty years, the esoteric aspect of Japanese gardening, particularly the Zen tradition, has caught the imagination of gardeners elsewhere. A group of rocks in a dry garden can symbolize Buddhist teaching, aid meditation or simply create a feeling of solidity and permanence. Though it might seem odd, there is a recognizable link between these austere, abstract gardens of rocks and sand and landscaped pond gardens, for if there is one thread that runs through the entire tradition of Japanese gardening during the last twelve centuries, it is a love of the diverse landscape of the Japanese islands: hills covered with pine forests and thickets of bamboo, valleys of golden rice fields, the open sea dotted with islands, the surf which rolls up on smooth, glistening sands or batters itself against a rocky coast. There is also an affection for each of the four seasons, which are clearly marked in the temperate marine climate of the country: the snows and frost of winter, the cheerful sunshine of spring, the sheen of water on leaves during the rainy month, the relentless glare of summer, the clear blue skies of autumn.

These are the elements constantly brought into the Japanese garden. From earliest times, formal gardens represented the mountains, woodlands and waterfalls, lakes, streams and open grassland of the natural world. In contrast to the image of a bower of flowers, Japanese gardens of all styles weave their rich tapestry in shades of green, emphasized by white gravel and the greenish-grey of rocks. Flowering trees, shrubs, perennials and annuals are used with great restraint, as are plants with berries or variegated leaves. Even the use of deciduous trees, including the fabulous Japanese maples which come in such a range of brilliant leaf colors, is generally restricted. Seasonal interest is concentrated on a small number of carefully selected and positioned plants of this kind. In practical terms, this means that Japanese gardens do not have an off-season during winter, since the rocks, the sand, the trained evergreens and conifers do not change. Winter brings no dug-up borders of bare earth, simply because in these traditional gardens there are no borders or beds in the western sense.

This is not to say that the Japanese are not passionate hybridizers of plants, mesmerized like people all over the world by the endless patterns and colors Nature seems capable of throwing up in the game of genetic roulette: countless prize cultivars of tree

peonies, morning glories, chrysanthemums and, more recently, calanthes have been coddled and cherished by enthusiasts. In the eighteenth century there was a craze for variegated camellias and mandarin oranges (*Citrus tachibana*) not unlike the tulipomania that

below: *This hill and pond garden in San Marino, California, follows the Japanese custom of creating a smooth, undulating contour to the land.*

overtook Europe in the previous century. Chrysanthemums were exhibited with just as much competitive pride as auriculas and pinks were in the north of England. These passions, however, are kept separate from the traditional art of garden-making.

Fancy cultivars of *Iris ensata*, for example, are more often grown in pots than planted out in the garden, so the large, showy blooms can easily be admired much closer at hand.

Perhaps the best way of capturing the spirit of Japanese gardens is not to attempt to grow rhododendrons and maples where they simply will not thrive, or to build vermilion bridges and tea-houses — not even necessarily to create waterfalls gushing over rocks — but to try to re-create a local landscape the gardener loves. It may be done with heathers in Scotland, for example. The important thing is to draw on the means of arriving at the special stillness and serenity which Japanese gardens exude, and use them like any other garden tool, instead of trying to reproduce faithful copies of a foreign land. The aim is to achieve an effect of controlled calm by emphasizing space, austere simplicity and shapes.

Changing gardening styles

Most of the terrain of Japan has acid soil, which largely determines the choice of garden plants there. Most are native species; others, such as the tree peony, flowering peaches and flowering crabapples, were highly prized Chinese shrubs brought to Japan in ancient times; still other shrubs, like *Mahonia japonica*, were Chinese medicinal plants imported into Japan in the seventeenth and eighteenth centuries. A handful of European and American plants have become firm favorites in Japan, especially broom and the American dogwoods. The Japanese describe their gardens as naturalistic, but they are not woodland or wild-flower gardens. Instead, a very careful selection of plants and rocks and stones encapsulates, refines and embodies the spirit of the local landscape for all to see and experience.

As more and more exotic plants arrive from overseas, garden styles are changing in Japan too. The fashion these days is for English-style gardens with lavender and old-fashioned roses, even though both tend to suffer in Japan's more humid climate. Fewer and fewer houses are being built in the traditional way with wood and wattle and daub; modern houses are made of prefabricated materials instead. Inside they have carpets, not thick straw mats; curtains, not sliding doors covered with rice-paper. For more than 1200 years, people in Japan sat on cushions on the floor; they gazed at their gardens from immaculately polished verandahs. Fifty years ago habits started to be westernized. Just as the furniture in the living-room is more likely these days to be sofas and coffee-tables, people are likely to look out on their gardens from a glass window or a patio door. Styles in both architecture and design change and develop. Gardens in Japan now tend to be brighter, with fewer somber evergreens and more lawn. There are more flowers too. But sometimes the old ways can remind us of a different way of thinking about gardens. For those unfamiliar with the techniques and concepts traditional to Japanese gardening, learning about these traditions may stimulate new approaches and help them to realize their own visions in the gardens.

The tradition of Japanese gardening stretches back 1400 years. Though different styles developed as the social functions of gardens changed, the underlying concept has stayed surprisingly consistent. The approach has always involved paring the natural world down to its essential elements to refine an understanding of the workings of both Nature and time. Gardens are often passed on from generation to generation like prized bonsai trees. They transcend time and fashion. Their shapes and forms take on a universal appeal which brings peace to those who inherit this art of gardening.

The four basic types of Japanese gardens are described in the next chapter: hill and pond gardens, dry gardens, tea gardens and courtyard gardens.

facing page: *This Swiss garden seems to extend to the very horizon, bounded only by the sky and the grey silhouettes of distant mountains. The Max Koch Garden succeeds in merging flawlessly together an intimate water garden planted with* Iris laevigata *and a panoramic view over the lake. The raised decking provides an ideal viewing platform, and the choice of natural materials for both the decking and the bridge prevents them from clashing with the overall feel of the garden.*

CHAPTER ONE

Traditional Japanese Gardens

The earliest descriptions of gardens in Japan are found in seventh-century poems. From them it is possible to see that lakes and islands and bridges were already the principal features of the aristocratic gardens of that period. Picturesque rocky shorelines were also being created to add variety to the landscape.

Right from the beginning, Japanese gardens were the products of a highly self-conscious culture which tried to recreate naturalistic landscapes near people's houses, but also to find pleasure in reminders of Nature's rugged and untamed wilderness.

The hill and pond garden

right: *A vermilion gateway forms a brilliant contrast to the deep blue Californian sky. Sequoias are combined with traditionally pruned pines in this San Francisco garden. The short trees and shrubs planted down the incline are neatly pruned, helping to create an impression of dense planting. A low embankment in a more informal garden can be planted with a single variety of a weeping bush such as Japanese bush clover (species of* Lespedeza) *which produces tiny purple-pink, pea-like blossoms in autumn.*

previous page: *An unpainted, ornamental bridge is well suited to a woodland setting. At the same time, well-groomed evergreen shrubs and azaleas provide the touch of formality a bridge of this type requires. Middle-sized pines, enkianthuses, and taller evergreen shrubs can be arranged together with ground-hugging junipers next to water. Conifers such as* Taxus cuspidata *and* Juniperus chinensis *have many dwarf forms which can be used in these situations. Prune the trees and shrubs carefully to keep their overall shape.*

The choice of landscapes to reproduce was closely connected with how people saw their country. By building islands in the middle of lakes they were confirming their identity as an island people. Gardens of this kind came to play an even greater role in aristocratic life once the imperial court was moved to Kyoto at the end of the eighth century. As this area was blessed with many springs, as well as being watered by several clear rivers issuing from the richly forested mountain ranges surrounding the city to the north, east and west of the broad valley floor, it is hardly surprising that lakes became more significant in gardens than ever before. About the time the first imperial palace in Kyoto was being constructed, a garden was built around a sacred spring just south of the palace grounds. This garden eventually included a large lake with a sacred island, overlooked by another palace. Later aristocratic gardens in Kyoto were modelled on this imperial prototype.

For the next four centuries, a highly sophisticated culture flourished in these garden palaces. This society gave birth, for example, to *The Tale of Genji*, a portrait of the life of refined and sensitive emotions led by the nobility. The author, Lady Murasaki Shikibu, lived at the end of the tenth century and the beginning of the eleventh. The exquisite feelings she described include responses to the natural world, though these reactions are kept within the conventions of the time. The court revolved around a strict calendar of elaborate rituals and splendid ceremonies, and it made great formal occasions of excursions to outlying hills in the autumn. There the nobility amused themselves by picking wild flowers which they then replanted in their gardens at home. Pilgrimages to more distant temples also provided rare opportunities for these aristocrats to leave the confines of the city. Along the way they were able to catch glimpses of white beaches, wind-tossed pines and the sea itself. These were the landscapes they wanted to have re-created for them in paintings and in their gardens.

A typical palace faced south and looked out on an open expanse of sand, a ritual space, beyond which might be some scattered planting, and then a large lake fed by a channel which was dug so that it ran into the garden from one corner of the estate, passing under several corridors of the palace on its way. This stream was embellished with rocks to

simulate a rippling brook, and around it the terrain was made to undulate gently. Here, the clumps of wild flowers gathered in the hills were replanted: balloon flowers, hostas, yellow valerian and bush clover. The nobility of Kyoto loved gentle, sloping mountains like the ones nearby. There were also older

memories of the perfectly shaped, dome-like mountains around the older capitals of Nara and Asuka – mountains immortalized in some of the oldest poetry in Japan. These "feminine" mountains are quite unlike the precipitous, craggy, dangerous mountains lying further to the east. After the

above: *A weeping willow is carefully positioned over a pond so that it casts its reflection in the water. Japanese maples are also often used in this way.*

opening of Japan to the West in the nineteenth century, these were called the Japan Alps.

The white, sparkling beaches that once surrounded the Bay of Osaka were copied in these grand gardens. For the sake of contrast, rocky shorelines were often built to represent Nature's wilder aspects. The lake would have up to three islands, all connected with bridges. During courtly entertainments, these islands provided an ideal stage for musicians, who also performed from gilded and painted boats. Guests would admire them from the palace verandah as they caught sight of them between the pine-trees. They would listen as the music wafted closer, then became more distant as the boats floated away. Another room from which the garden could be seen was an open one built directly over the lake and connected to the rest of the house by a long corridor. From here, or from a separate pier, elegant princes and their ladies were able to go out on the cool lake on fierce summer days.

Temple and palace gardens

Sadly, none of these palace gardens has survived the centuries in anything like their original shape, but there are other lake gardens in the grounds of Buddhist temples. As they were intended to evoke an idea of the paradise Buddha was thought to inhabit, they are referred to as paradise gardens. In these gardens, the main hall of the temple is built facing the lake. From this hall, the statue of Buddha gazes serenely over his tranquil domain where the sacred lotus flowers bloom.

In the twelfth century, political power began to shift to the warrior classes. Architectural fashions began to evolve too, reflecting the provincial, even rural background of many of the new warlords. Some of the most powerful of them became Buddhist monks in later life, and this meant that features taken from monastic buildings were also used in many of the villas and retreats they commissioned. Many gardens lost the open ritual space of swept sand which formerly divided the house from the lake. Rocks gradually began to be more prominent in the landscape. Lonely outcrops of stone appeared in the middle of garden lakes, and they were increasingly identified with sacred mountains in Buddhist and Chinese mythology. Paths were planned to allow these gardens to be seen from different directions, and the stroll garden came into being.

Water, buildings, rocks, moss, trees, shrubs: all had their part to play in creating the complex effect of these gardens. With the development of the tea garden in the sixteenth and seventeeth centuries, new influences were swiftly absorbed into the design of stroll gardens, and what was intimate and modest in the tea garden became grand and ambitious. It was around that time that the famous imperial gardens belonging to the Katsura and Shugakuin Palaces near Kyoto were built. At Katsura, stepping-stones, paths and bridges meander among five large and small islands. In one place, a pebbly spit of land juts out into the lake, its point adorned with a single round stone lantern standing on an outcrop of rock like a miniature lighthouse. This headland was thought to represent a celebrated landscape on the coast of the Sea of Japan, known as the Bridge to Heaven. The route around the garden at Katsura dips into shady glens and rises again towards a fanciful mountain pass, where there is a humble building like a mountain inn. As well as holding several landscapes in miniature, Katsura is also a tea garden, leading guests up to any one of the seven tea-houses within the grounds. There are the usual features of a well-appointed tea garden: roofed benches for meeting people, stone lanterns along the pathways, and basins of water for washing hands. The palace complex itself stands imposingly in the middle of an open expanse of lawn. With its clean, strong

left: *These standing stones surrounded by a birch forest carpeted with soft moss look ancient. Japanese gardens strive to attain this timeless quality but it does take patience to achieve it. There is certainly quiet enjoyment to be savored in planning how a garden will look to future generations.*

below: *Azaleas and Iris ensata in bloom together in the East Garden of the Imperial Palace in Tokyo. The irises here are planted in marshy ground and their informal drifts form a pleasing contrast with the pruned azaleas.*

facing page: *Shrubs such as Pieris japonica, box-leaved holly (Ilex crenata), and azaleas can be planted among rocks to fill out awkward corners and soften their lines. Their shapes should be controlled so as to complement the rocks, not overwhelm them.*

lines and austere simplicity, it forms another dramatic feature of the garden.

For the next two centuries, following this high point in the history of gardens in Japan, the stroll garden remained the status symbol of the highest-ranking noblemen in the country and a significant drain on their purses. The construction of elaborate stroll gardens was expected of a feudal lord as an

indication of his peaceful intentions. It was another way for the overlord of the whole country, the shogun in Edo (Tokyo), to make sure his vassals' finances were so thoroughly drained that they would never have enough spare money to organize a successful revolt. However, the tradition stagnated and became rigidly formulaic, until the entire culture of the warrior class collapsed when Japan was finally forced to open her doors to the western world in the middle of the nineteenth century.

Man-made hills

In the West, gardeners often go to a great deal of trouble to level the ground for a smooth lawn. In Japan, manuals teach how to add contours to flat land to give added depth and perspective to a garden. If a pond or a small lake is being made, the earth removed during its construction is ideally suited for building small mounds, hills or knolls to produce a gently undulating landscape.

Japanese gardens tend not to be densely planted, and the gardens of Kyoto had expanses of open ground. The idea is not to cover the entire mound with shrubs or perennials but to leave open spaces. A mound can be embellished with a group of stones halfway up its slope, with a few azalea bushes or perhaps a sprawling juniper. Ground-cover can be varied: swathes of *Ophiopogon*, with their distinct strap-like leaves, show up well against a background of moss, or broad stretches of neatly trimmed, low hedging plants – azaleas or bamboo grasses – might form a contrast with open, grassy areas. Larger knolls are suitable for arrangements of taller trees. Where a garden seeks to re-create a wooded hillside, round pruned bushes and trees of differing heights can be used to produce an impression of wave upon wave of greenery.

On flatter terrain, trees of the same species can be planted to suggest the idea of a forest, but by clearing away the undergrowth, except for clumps of woodland perennials here and there to direct the eye, a sense of spaciousness can be produced at the same time. Another trick is to plant a tall shrub or tree near the principal vantage-point. In Japan, a popular choice for such a position is *Osmanthus fragrans* f. *aurantiacus*, the fragrant olive, which bears clusters of intensely sweet orange flowers in the autumn. In this way, it is possible to enjoy the feeling of being surrounded by lush vegetation without actually overcrowding the garden. Using tall, top-heavy trees alone will naturally emphasize their height. If this threatens to overbalance the garden, the introduction of shorter but shapely shrubs, or a stone basin or lantern, will help to give more stability to the group.

For an artificial hill, first dig the site to the depth of 12 in (30 cm) or more in order to loosen the compacted topsoil. The earth for the mound is added in tiers 12 in (30 cm) deep, each one firmed down thoroughly before the next is added. A rod marked with the desired height of the mound will be useful in the center, but it is a good idea to add a little extra earth since the mound will inevitably sink as it settles. The slope of the mound should be at an angle of between 35 and 45 degrees. The last step is to smooth the surface of the mound and plant it with suitable ground-cover to stabilize it.

Designing hill and pond gardens

The large garden: In a large garden, it may be possible to create a varied landscape with low hills, a lake, and islands linked to the rest of the garden by bridges. It is largely a question of proportion, but a lot also depends on the mood the gardener wants to achieve. To preserve a sense of open space, it might be best to have a simple island with only rocks and maybe a solitary pine-tree. This will give a view of the opposite bank beyond the island, a shoreline not heavily planted but kept plain with a shingle or pebble beach. A garden that is more densely planted would require an island that reflects the same approach, with more color, perhaps including the use of painted bridges.

This type of garden has something in common with the great English landscape gardens of the eighteenth century. Since the aim is to represent Nature as seen and refined through the imagination, it is better to avoid highly hybridized cultivars, especially flowering shrubs with blooms of stronger, modern colors, and also to keep plants with variegated leaves at a minimum. When they are strategically placed, one or two trees or shrubs of this kind can catch the eye and introduce light to a dark corner, but too many of them will only diminish the effect and be distracting. This is true of bronze-leaved trees and shrubs as well. They are apt to bring autumn into the garden too early unless there is plenty of lush, green foliage around to form a contrast.

A Japanese-style garden of this sort would not be difficult to integrate into a larger, western-type landscape garden. While fences and walls play an important role in other Japanese styles, stroll gardens have such a degree of affinity with landscape gardening generally that a wall separating a Japanese area from the rest of the garden might actually seem an unnecessary barrier. The attraction of a Japanese garden is its sense of being a special place, and a garden in any kind of foreign style is going to be special by virtue of its own difference. This special place does not have to be defined by a wall. The secret to creating a successful Japanese garden within a larger scheme lies in the choice of the site: perhaps

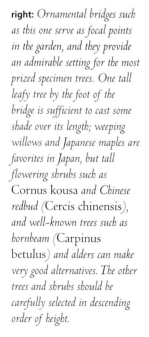

right: Ornamental bridges such as this one serve as focal points in the garden, and they provide an admirable setting for the most prized specimen trees. One tall leafy tree by the foot of the bridge is sufficient to cast some shade over its length; weeping willows and Japanese maples are favorites in Japan, but tall flowering shrubs such as Cornus kousa *and Chinese redbud (*Cercis chinensis*), and well-known trees such as hornbeam (*Carpinus betulus*) and alders can make very good alternatives. The other trees and shrubs should be carefully selected in descending order of height.*

a secluded out-of-the-way dell, where a mysterious pond might be just right. A toadstool-shaped lantern of natural, uncut stone can help to signpost the area. On the other hand, all expectations can be confounded by boldly letting a spacious vista open out where the visitor least expects it. Japan is a densely forested country with many swift streams and tranquil mountain pools. It is this intimate presence of Nature which Japanese gardens try to capture.

All over the world people are attracted to Japanese styles of gardening because they produce a sense of tranquillity, even of spirituality. The effect is seldom attributable simply to the use of particular religious imagery, whether it be statues of Buddha or a *torii*, the gate made of a horizontal beam and a lintel supported on two pillars, which serves as the gateway to a Shinto shrine. It is more often a cumulative effect of the design of the entire garden. The key to the Japanese idea of spirituality is this sense of a sacred space, a space which is separate and distinct from the mundane, everyday realm of existence. An island in the middle of a lake can become a sacred space; so can a Zen rock garden and even a tea garden. But this special space can also occur in the middle of a commercial building in the form of an indoor garden – or in a back garden, through the use of

above: *A beach of fine white gravel edging a pond re-creates in miniature the image of a broad seashore of sparkling sand and windswept pines. Rocks, pebbles, and gravel of differing sizes, textures, and colors are used effectively here, for example, to give a feeling of depth to the stream. Rocks and big stones look more solid and permanent if they are embedded in the ground as they always are in Japan. This garden, designed by Peter Chan and Brenda Sacoor, is in Weybridge, Surrey, England.*

fencing. By shutting out the external world, a garden can both help to concentrate and enlarge the mind. This idea of a sacred space is not particularly foreign to the West. Sacred trees, rocks and wells are found all over Europe, and sacred spaces act as a focus for the awe which Nature as a whole can inspire in us.

A *torii* gate usually marks out the sacred precincts of a Shinto shrine. The propriety of putting *torii* gates in western gardens is perhaps questionable; even from the sole consideration of proportion and harmony in the garden, a full-sized *torii* gate actually needs a shrine building to counterbalance its somewhat ponderous presence. It is after all a gate, and gates lead somewhere, but an island in a lake could be given an inconspicuous, smaller *torii* gate to indicate its sacred status. An acceptable alternative is a small household shrine; many traditional Japanese gardens used to include these shrines, which were no more than about 3 ft (90 cm) or so high, with a small vermilion *torii* in front of them. But it cannot be emphasized enough that these shrines are objects of worship. The same can be said for statues of Buddha. Stones engraved with a bodhisattva, a holy spirit, are often found by ancient roads in Japan. These, too, are objects of veneration and are usually tended affectionately by local people.

The smaller garden: In a small garden, it might be too ambitious to have both a pond and hills, but there are several alternatives which draw upon the various traditional styles of gardening. One option is to dedicate most of the garden to a large pond, preferably a shallow one, surrounded by very low ground-cover – moss or *Ophiopogon*, varied with liriope or ferns; several low-growing, shade-tolerant shrubs with berries such as *Ardisia japonica* (marlberry), *Aucuba japonica* (spotted laurel), or the taller *Osmanthus heterophyllus* (Chinese holly); and then a few trees with their lower branches carefully

removed. The trees will then form a delightful canopy. A different feeling altogether is achieved when the surrounding banks of the pond are planted quite densely with round, pruned azalea bushes, interspersed with a few maples, clipped pines and rocks, maybe with a lantern. This kind of planting is even more effective if the ground rises towards the back of the garden, conveying the impression of a wooded hillside.

Experiment with different levels of planting in the garden. The contrast of texture between low

ground-cover and a broad swathe of clipped shrubs, for example azaleas, *Sasa veitchii* (bamboo grass) or *Photinia glabra* (an evergreen with attractive red leaf-buds), that continues down the far side of a mound can be very attractive. Another effective technique for creating a feeling of distance is to plant a tree on the far side of a slope, so that only part of it is visible from the house. This will help to create an illusion that there is more to the garden, tucked away out of sight. The technique of partly hiding garden features – whether it is a tree, a waterfall or a stone lantern –

facing page: Selaginella kraussiana *makes a good alternative to moss, and since it belongs to the fern family, it goes well with other members of that group of plants. They thrive in areas with high humidity where they produce lush growth. The rock protruding from the surface of the pond is of a type often used in Japan because it is thought to resemble a carp raising its head out of the water.*

above: *The atmosphere of a mountain retreat is created by this rustic gateway and the simplest style of bamboo fencing, the* yotsume, *which lines the entrance pathway. The contrasting colors and textures of the gravel, the chipped bark, moss and the black-leaved* Ophiopogon planiscapus *"Nigrescens" produce an agreeable sense of formality and quiet dignity in this Washington garden.*

right: *The sliding doors of a room open to reveal a hill and pond garden in this city residence belonging to the Iwasa family, one of the priestly families serving the ancient Kamigamo Shrine in Kyoto.*

Ponds, streams and rills can be constructed close to a house provided that they pose no threat to the foundations of the building. Since Japanese houses are traditionally built with the floors raised 18 inches (45 cm) off the ground, it is possible to look out over the pond from inside the room.

Pruned azaleas, box-leaved holly (Ilex crenata) and rocks fill in the space in the foreground, allowing the eye to descend gradually to the level of the pond. The bank at the back of the garden rises steeply and a rock is strategically positioned so it will be at eye-level when seen from the room, producing an illusion of depth and distance.

is very important in Japanese gardens. It not only creates a sense of distance in a smaller garden, but it encourages the visitors to the garden to use their imagination. A tree or shrub that is half-glimpsed is considered extremely attractive. If the garden is too densely planted with many different kinds of perennials and shrubs, this effect will be lost.

Sloping ground can be combined with a meandering brook toward the bottom end of the garden, along with some trees. This will leave a patch of open ground nearer the house, which can be embellished with stepping stones, a lantern or rocks; or clumps of ferns, a *Fatsia japonica*, or low-growing shrubs. Perennials such as astilbe, with its frothy pink plumes that contrast so well with the dark green leaves, and *Filipendula purpurea*, which also form attractive clumps with feathery flowers, are ideal for planting next to small streams. Around limpid pools and basins of water, choose the delicate nodding flowers of *Begonia grandis* subsp. *evansiana*.

Traditional houses in Japan invariably possessed a wide verandah which was separated from the neighboring rooms by sliding doors fitted with paper screens. The garden could be enjoyed either from the verandah or, when the sliding doors were fully open, from the rooms inside, when the entire breadth of the garden could be seen. A similar effect can be achieved with a glass wall, which can diminish the sense of a barrier existing between house and garden. One way of capturing the feel of a verandah is to build a wooden terrace or deck above the level of the rest of the garden. Japanese houses are still raised off the ground in order to keep the woodwork properly aired during the humid summers. Traditionally, a large stone was placed near the verandah to serve as a step down into the garden. Wooden steps can serve a similar purpose. A terrace of this kind would also provide a space for entertaining, which traditional Japanese gardens lack.

Plants for different situations

Planting along the back of the perimeter of a large garden: *Cryptomeria japonica, Tsuga sieboldii* (southern Japanese hemlock).

Specimen tree for a mound: pines, *Podocarpus macrophylla* (yew pine), *Diospyros kaki* (Japanese persimmon), *Chamaecyparis obtusa* (hinoki), *Ilex crenata* (box-leaved holly), *I. integra, Taxus cuspidata* var. *nana* (dwarf yew), *Ternstroemia gymnanthera, Sciadopitys verticillata* (Japanese umbrella pine), *Magnolia grandiflora.*

Accompaniment for specimen trees or on islands in the middle of ponds: *Pinus parviflora* (Japanese white pine), *Ilex crenata* (box-leaved holly), *Taxus cuspidata* var. *nana* (dwarf yew), *Ilex integra,* Japanese maples.

Underplanting for specimen trees: *Selaginella tamariscina, Farfugium japonicum, Pieris japonica* (Japanese andromeda).

Underplanting for deciduous trees: *Erythronium japonicum* (Japanese trout-lily), *Tricyrtis hirta* (toad lily).

Weeping trees for the pond-side: pines, *Podocarpus macrophyllus* (yew pine), *Juniperus chinensis, Taxus cuspidata* var. *nana* (dwarf yew), weeping cultivars of willow and cherry.

By ponds and lakes: *Albizia julibrissin* (silk tree), Japanese maples, *Taxus cuspidata* var. *nana* (dwarf yew), *Ilex serrata* (Japanese winterberry), *Juniperus chinensis, Hydrangea* spp., *Malus floribunda* (Japanese crab), *Euonymus alatus, Corylopsis pauciflora* (buttercup witch hazel), *Rhododendron reticulatum* and other spp., *Callicarpa japonica* (Japanese beauty-berry), *Spiraea thunbergii;* "wild" flowers: *Reineckea carnea, Cypripedium japonicum* (lady's slipper), *Equisetum hiemale* (scouring rush, horsetail).

In front of a waterfall: evergreens, Japanese maples, weeping willow.

Above a waterfall: oaks, *Osmanthus fragrans* f. *aurantiacus* (fragrant olive), *Ilex integra,* evergreens (but not conifers).

Downstream: *Acorus gramineus* (Japanese rush), *Pieris japonica* (Japanese andromeda), *Equisetum hiemale* (horsetail), *Eurya japonica, Iris ensata, I. laevigata.*

To prevent erosion of earth around streams and ponds: *Acorus gramineus* (Japanese rush).

By a bridge: weeping willow, Japanese maples.

For the east end of a south-facing garden: evergreens with beautiful leaves such as pines, *Tsuga sieboldii* (Japanese hemlock), *Cryptomeria japonica* (Japanese cedar), *Ternstroemia gymnanthera.*

For the west end of a south-facing garden: flowering shrubs generally, Japanese maples, flowering cherries, *Prunus mume* (Japanese apricot).

On an embankment: *Juniperus chinensis, Lespedeza* spp., *Spiraea cantoniensis* (Reeves's spiraea), azaleas, *Ophiopogon japonicus.*

Among trees planted on a slope: bamboo grasses such as *Sasa veitchii* and *Shibataea kumasasa, Iris japonica.*

"Wild" flowers as underplanting for shrubs and shorter trees (*nejime*): *Platycodon grandiflorum* (balloon flower), *Hosta* spp., *Ajuga nipponensis* (Japanese bugle), *Cymbidium goeringii, Ardisia japonica.*

facing page: *Aristocratic houses in ninth- and tenth-century Kyoto possessed rooms built over the garden lake. This garden creates a similar effect with decking, which forms a viewing platform over the water. The pond is not actually very large, but the use of tall shrubs at the far end of the pool creates the illusion of depth.*

The dry garden

right: *Native American firs provide a backdrop for this dry garden at the Japanese Garden in Portland, Oregon. It is edged in the traditional manner with round azaleas. The fine white gravel is raked to suggest ripples of water, while a flat rock reinforces the illusion that the expanse of sand is a lake.*

facing page: *The garden at Ryoan-ji Temple in Kyoto is perhaps the most well-known yet enigmatic of the austere Zen rock and sand gardens. Created in the seventeenth century, it is considered by some literal-minded connoisseurs of later periods to represent a mother tiger protecting her cubs from a panther, though the only true interpretation remains in the eyes of each beholder.*

In the fourteenth century, Buddhist monks, including some very eminent Zen priests, were already involved in designing temple gardens with groups of dry rocks representing various Zen concepts and Buddhist imagery. These early clusters of rocks stood on the gently undulating slopes of hill and pond gardens. Unlike the more austere stone and sand gardens of later periods, these gardens were not completely dry but often still contained ponds or springs and were lush and green. Even though the rocks were symbolic, it was still important that they should look as if they had naturally come to rest where they lay.

Dry rock gardens grew in popularity, especially among temples which were not so well supplied with water, until in the seventeenth century there was a reform of temple regulations, and the south garden, which faced the meditation hall of the abbot's residence, fell out of use for important religious rituals. These areas were transformed into flat dry gardens featuring the white sand or gravel with which they had originally been covered. These new gardens sometimes included moss, shrubs and pine-trees, but they had no water. The mountains and rivers which had always been components of traditional gardens were now represented in abstract and motionless forms – in groups of rocks suggesting waterfalls, and sand swept into patterns which stylized the appearance of currents. Thus these gardens became truly dry. They perfectly suited the discipline of Zen sects, for the abstract shapes helped to exercise the mind, and the gardens became an aid to meditation on time, eternity, transience and permanence.

Laid out on flat, rectangular areas, often clearly demarcated (and separated from the outer world) by a fence, a mud wall or a tall hedge, these gardens pursued the ideal of capturing what is eternally unchanging. Dry gardens, like many other Japanese types of gardens, have a feeling of unworldliness, which, in their case, is emphasized by the wall that often surrounds them. They were designed to be looked at from the verandah of the monastery building. No one descends into the garden except to sweep it. It is not a casual construction. Shallow and wide, it faces the entire length of the biggest hall in the abbot's residence, and when all the sliding doors are wide open, it can be seen in full, forming an integral part of the priest's quarters. Where trees and shrubs are included in the design, they are severely pruned to preserve always the same shape. Beautiful

round azalea bushes can symbolize the idea of perfection or represent Buddha's disciples gathered
round him – Buddha, the Enlightened One, being
represented by a single, solid boulder.

Daisen-in, a subsidiary temple of Daitoku-ji, a
Zen temple in Kyoto, possesses one of the most
elaborate symbolic rock gardens. The rocks are
arranged to represent a dry waterfall tumbling down
the side of a vast mountain. At the bottom, a bridge

of rock spans a craggy gorge. A narrow mountain
stream, represented by a band of sand, winds its
tourtuous way among the rocks until it eventually
broadens into a wide river on which a boat-shaped
stone sails. On one side of the waterfall stand two
tall boulders, representing a ridge of mountains.
These are not the gentle mountains of Japan, but the
jagged, precipitous mountains depicted in Chinese
scroll paintings of the Sung period (960–1279).

next page: *Dry gardens can be
adapted to fit the smallest spaces,
with green areas planted to
simulate shorelines and islands.
Keep the planting to a minimum; suitable trees include
Japanese maples, pines, and
Stewartia pseudocamellia,
often planted in Zen gardens.
For still smaller gardens, foliage
plants, ferns, azaleas and shorter
bamboos are good choices.*

This style of painting became well-known and popular in Japan, especially among Zen priests for whom calligraphy was both an important discipline and an art form. At the same time, the rock on the right is identified with Fudo-myoo, Acala in Sanskrit, the Buddhist god of fire, the punisher of all evil, while the one on the left is identified with Kannon, the goddess of mercy. As this temple belongs to a Zen sect of Buddhism, there is also a low, flat-topped boulder representing a seat used by a priest practising meditation. The garden also contains groups of rocks representing a turtle and a crane, both auspicious creatures in Chinese Taoist mythology, which was introduced to Japan in the fourth to fifth centuries along with Buddhism. Fifteen turtles were believed to support a Mountain of Eternal Youth, where holy sages who had attained everlasting life flew on the backs of cranes.

Imagery from yet another religion can be seen in the gardens belonging to Zuiho-in, another of Daitoku-ji's subsidiary temples. This temple is known to have been founded by a medieval warlord who later converted to Christianity (which was introduced to Japan by St Francis Xavier in the middle of the sixteenth century). In one of its courtyards there is a seventeenth-century lantern in the *oribe* style, the bulges under the lantern box giving it a vague resemblance to the shape of a cross. The faint figure carved on the half-buried shaft is said to be the Virgin Mary. One of its twentieth-century gardens contains a group of stones which can be traditionally interpreted as representing the Mountain of Eternal Youth, the sacred home of Chinese sages; it also suggests an image of Christ's Sermon on the Mount, recorded in Matthew's Gospel.

Some gardens became less and less representative or symbolic, and increasingly austere and abstract, finally eliminating everything except sand, rocks and a little moss. Ryoan-ji Temple in Kyoto is the best

known example of this type. This garden is 39 ft (12 m) wide and 78 ft (24 m) long, and consists of fifteen rocks altogether, arranged in five groups: one group of five rocks, two of two rocks and two groups of three. Although water is suggested by patterns raked in the sand, the interpretation of the groups of rocks is ultimately left to the viewer. The rock garden at Ryoan-ji is deceptively simple; it is a garden that does not give up its secrets easily, for it is executed in the most abstract and esoteric of all styles of Japanese gardening. Gardens of this type depend absolutely on the quality – the beauty and the form – of each individual stone.

above: *Fine raked gravel or smooth pebbles arranged in an overlapping pattern create the impression of a flowing stream.*
This path at Ryoan-ji Temple in Kyoto is designed in the form of a stream-bed. Two stone slabs serve as a bridge over real water.

left: *The gravel used in dry gardens does not have to be white, although it is more challenging to create a contrast of light and darkness using gravel of more somber colors.*

This rooftop garden in New York, designed by Jeff Mendoza, is based on a theme of cool grey-blues and bright greens. In the corner a Japanese white pine with blue-green needles links the two thematic colors together.

above: *Large flat foundation stones from ruined temple buildings were treasured and lovingly reused in dry gardens and tea gardens. One of these circular stones in a Zen temple garden serves as an image of perfection and wholeness, while also acting as a reminder of the faith of past generations and of the passage of time. Here at Silverstream in Weybridge, two stones have been used for a similar effect, their smoothness forming a contrast with the jagged upright rocks. The con- centric circles raked into the gravel around them suggest calmness and order emanating from the center of the universe.*

Designing a dry garden

Dry gardens do not necessarily have to be flat. Groups of rocks can be situated on "islands" in the sand; these "islands" can consist of mounds of earth stabilized with moss or *Ophiopogon*. A larger mound, often in the form of a turtle island with a leaning rock representing the turtle's head and neck, can be planted with a pine-tree, the tree of sages, its banks indicated by more stones. Islands in a sea of sand can be suggested not only in this way by the use of rocks,

below: The bright gravel lights up the orange tones of this superb example of a Japanese maple. The "Dissectum" group of maples (Acer palmatum), to which this tree belongs, includes popular bronze-leaved cultivars, but others have leaves which subtly change color throughout spring, summer and autumn.

facing page: Basalt stepping-stones form a path across a "sea" of white gravel up to the entrance of a teahouse. A yarai-style fence with diagonal struts separates the yard from the road beyond. Ritsurin Park in Takamatsu on the island of Shikoku is one of the most famous of the hill and pond parks created by feudal lords in the eighteenth century.

but also with closely pruned, rounded shrubs such as azaleas and the dwarf yew, *Taxus cuspidata* var. *nana*.

A stream or river-bed of pebbles can help to add interesting contours to the dry garden. When the pebbles are laid out so that they slightly overlap each other like the scales of a fish, they can cleverly suggest the flow of the current. Choose the pebbles carefully for their color and sheen. Slabs of rock can serve as bridges over these imaginary brooks.

Larger areas of land can be represented by solidly planted bamboo grass, box-leaved holly, or *Photinia glabra*, cropped low. Wild flowers too can be incorporated into the garden design, growing in clumps on islands of moss, but smaller Japanese gardens tend to be very minimalist in the number of different plants they use. The basic tone of green in a garden is varied through the use of plants with different textures — springy moss and leathery-leaved camellias, for instance — and through the imaginative placing of clipped shrubs.

Paths are only one way in which a garden can be subtly divided into different areas. An area of white gravel can form a startling contrast with a swathe of moss or low, clipped bamboo grass, but the two areas can be made to harmonize with each other if the line of division is made sinuous rather than straight and harsh. This is particularly effective in gardens which are not flat but undulating. Low trees and shrubs are commonly used in all types of Japanese gardens as a kind of screen that partly conceals a section of the garden from view. Low partition fences and sleeve fences are used for a similar purpose in the smallest gardens, including dry ones.

In dry gardens, the ground-cover — whether it is moss or *Ophiopogon*, or even thyme or chamomile — must make a distinct contrast with the sand or gravel areas. This means that the sand or gravel must be kept clean and not allowed to get muddy or green and slimy with algae. Hosing down the sand and raking it afresh is part of the regular cleansing ritual of a Zen temple. It is admittedly easier to keep sand clean in a hot climate than in a wet, cold one, but the effort is what counts.

Plants in a dry garden

This may sound paradoxical, but dry gardens do not have to be devoid of plants, or indeed of color. Shrubs and trees as diverse as camellias, tree peonies, *Prunus mume* (Japanese apricot), flowering cherries,

crape myrtle, *Ardisia crispa*, and grasses such as *Miscanthus sinensis* will all do very well if there is adequate rain or they are watered when necessary. Azaleas in spring add a note of vibrancy to a garden with their range of soft pinks through to magenta-purples. A particular season can be suggested evocatively by a careful selection of one or more perennials in well-defined clumps: the fiery orange of double-flowered day lilies, *Hemerocallis fulva*, or the purple balloon flower, *Platycodon grandiflorum*.

Choose the accent plants with conviction, for they make a statement about what the gardener feels about the season – the intensity of summer heat or the calm regrets of autumn.

The care of moss

Moss is guaranteed to grow in the middle of your prized lawn, but it will stubbornly refuse to appear where the gardener wants it to thrive. Moss dislikes direct sunlight, preferring the more gentle light of morning or dappled shade. It also requires moisture. In Kyoto, where the most famous moss gardens are found, late afternoon showers are not unusual through spring and summer. In areas where the weather cannot be relied upon to provide this essential moisture, it is a good idea to give the moss a very light watering in the early evening. Try to avoid using tap water directly, for it contains harsh chemicals and minerals. Allow it to stand for two or three days before using it. Although moss needs moisture, it will not grow in ground which is saturated with water. The soil should be free-draining, and preferably sandy. Shady trees, bamboos and hedges in a moss garden help to block the wind which can dry the air. Moss should be protected from frost by covering it with pine needles or straw. This winter protection can become an appealing garden feature in its own right. If Japanese mosses are not available, Irish moss is a good substitute.

Other plants for the dry garden and the moss garden

Wide single hedges or tall ground-cover: *Castanopsis cuspidata, Cleyera japonica, Eurya japonica*, azaleas, *Shibataea kumasasa*.

Specimen trees: *Pinus parviflora, P. thunbergii, Cycas revoluta, Stewartia pseudocamellia*.

Tall hedges: *Lithocarpus edulis, Ligustrum japonicum* (Japanese privet), *Quercus dentata* (daimio oak), *Eurya emarginata*.

"Wild" flowers: spring: *Iris japonica*; summer: *Hemerocallis* spp. (day lilies); late summer: *Astilbe* spp., *Platycodon grandiflorum* (balloon flower), *Tricyrtis hirta* (toad lily); autumn: Japanese anemones, *Farfugium japonicum, Aster tartaricus, Liriope muscari, Physalis alkekengi* (Chinese lantern, winter cherry).

Bamboos and grasses: *Chimonobambusa quadrangularis, Phyllostachys nigra, P. sulphurea; Miscanthus sinensis* (eulalia, Chinese silvergrass).

Ground-cover: *Ophiopogon japonicus, Saxifraga stolonifera*.

Shrubs: *Eurya japonica, Citrus tachibana* (mandarin orange), *Juniperus chinensis* var. *procumbens, Zanthoxylum piperitum* (Japan pepper), *Camellia japonica* (common camellia), *C. sasanqua*, flowering cherries, *Prunus mume* (Japanese apricot), *Forsythia suspensa, Rhododendron japonicum, R. quinquefolium, R. reticulatum*, azaleas, *Cornus kousa, Lagerstroemia indica, Lespedeza* spp. (Japanese bush clover).

By a large plant pot: *Pieris japonica, Euonymus alatus, Taxus cuspidata* var. *nana* (dwarf yew), *Torreya nucifera* (Japanese nutmeg yew), *Ilex serrata, Aspidistra elatior, Farfugium japonicum, Iris japonica*.

The tea garden

The Japanese tea ceremony had its inception in the fifteenth century as a social entertainment devised by the Zen monk Shoko, who was under the patronage of the shogun, the overlord of the entire country, Ashikaga Yoshimasa (1436–90). A stylized ritual of preparing and drinking green tea with one's guests, it was quickly elevated to an art form through the genius of a succession of disciples, most notably by Sen-no-Rikyu in the sixteenth century, who championed the aesthetic principles of *wabi* and *sabi*, which involved simplicity, tranquillity, solitude and the dignity of age. In a time of great civil upheaval, Rikyu became a tea master to two of the most powerful and charismatic warlords of the period in succession. In the battle of wills on which he embarked with the second of them, Toyotomi Hideyoshi (1537–98), who had succeeded in subjugating the whole of feudal, war-torn Japan under his rule, Rikyu was to stamp his own strong personality on the tea ceremony forever. His preference for humble, rustic, weathered surroundings for his tea ceremonies was a direct challenge to Hideyoshi's love of ostentatious displays of power and wealth – he travelled with a personal tea set made of gold. Rikyu modelled his tea-rooms on the traditional image of the forest hermitage, the thatched single-room retreats of Buddhist hermits who had eschewed the world. The sole surviving example of his tea-rooms is barely more than 6 ft² (1.8 m²) in size, the walls made of straw mixed with cow dung. Although close to other temple buildings, it is reached only through the garden. Guests were expected to lay aside their swords and sit side by side, soldier and merchant, in mutual enjoyment of tranquillity and tea.

The garden has an important part to play in preparing guests for the tea ceremony. Laid out as an approach to the tea-room or tea-house, the garden includes a sequence of features, each of which is designed with some purpose in mind to help guests purify themselves, both body and soul, in readiness for the enjoyment of tea. This type of garden is generally known in Japanese as a "passageway" garden (*roji*). It is traditionally divided into two sections – the outer and the inner garden – each separated from the other by a hedge or a fence, and a gate. A covered shelter with benches provided with round, woven seat-mats is usually situated in the outer garden for waiting guests. Here they are able to pause and meet each other before going forward to greet their host. Passing through the inner gate, they leave behind the chaotic bustle of worldly existence. Hence, in some tea gardens this inner gate is nothing

more than a square opening cut into a mud wall; the guests must crouch in order to pass through it. But the inner gate can also be simple and rustic, constructed of roughly hewn timber and logs, with or without a gabled roof of thatch or shingles. A gate of this kind is meant to create the impression of a forest retreat. The urban tea garden seeks to re-create a deep forest setting in the city.

The tea garden is made more enjoyable by subtly changing the mood between the outer and the inner garden. The outer garden can be bolder in design, perhaps with larger stepping-stones, or a formal six-sided *kasuga* stone lantern. Alternatively, it can be given rocks with contrasting shapes, textures and

above: *A Japanese effect can be produced using local materials instead of bamboo. A simple Western-style wooden fence is combined here with a gateway of Japanese design (Riverwood, Portland, Oregon).*

colors, and in this way can be made more abstract than the inner garden. The planting scheme should also be subtly different in the two main divisions of the garden. The inner garden can be planted up to suggest a type of forest, pine or maple, for example. But this is not to say that these gardens are like the naturalistic woodland gardens of the West. A select number of plants creates the illusion of many. The variety of different kinds of plants is carefully restricted to the bare minimum necessary to produce the desired image of sylvan solitude. Trees, shrubs and clumps of ferns or grasses are juxtaposed with each other seemingly without any order or sense — they are not arranged according to height, nor do they form anything resembling a border or an island bed. The ground-cover of moss, liriope or *Ophiopogon*, or even a patchwork of these, forms, as it were, the forest undergrowth through which stepping-stones pick a path around groups of shrubs and clumps of ferns. The ground-cover comes right up to the base of the plants. Never are many different shrubs thrown together in one group. The basic idea, common to all the different kinds of Japanese gardens, is that each plant in the garden should be capable of being appreciated for its own shape and form — not necessarily from a single angle. The meandering track of stepping-stones helps produce unexpected perspectives and surprises.

The tea garden is not intended to be looked at from the tea-room, although a few early tea masters daringly placed rocks and lanterns so that they could only be seen from the tea-house window. Once the guest enters the special space of the tea-room, the garden is left behind with the rest of the world. Just as the tea ceremony focuses on what is immediate, each stepping-stone, which carefully measures the speed with which guests stroll through the garden, helps them attune themselves to the present moment.

The tea garden is, above all, a functional space.

The principle behind it is to have everything immaculately prepared so that guests can be welcomed hospitably, naturally, and seemingly effortlessly. There might be tiny bridges consisting of a single slab of stone to help suggest a forest rill. A low stone basin suggests a cool mountain spring or brook, by which guests need to crouch in order to refresh themselves, washing their hands and rinsing their mouths just as people do at shrines and temples. Many traditional basins are stoups hewn out of a piece of natural rock. In former times, a piece of

carved stone rescued from the ruins of a temple or salvaged from a wrecked lantern was sometimes reshaped as a basin, a practice encouraged by Rikyu himself; similarly, old disused lanterns from shrines or temples were used in tea gardens before tea masters began designing their own. A more geometrically regular, round basin, based on the design of a coin, or a square one with bas reliefs of Buddha

facing page: *In this garden, designed by Marc Peter Keane, granite slabs and millstones are combined to create a path leading up to the inconspicuous entrance to a tea-house. A slightly raised, flat stone acts as a step up to the tiny porch. The projecting cedar bark sleeve fence to the right partly conceals the tea-house from view.*

above: *A flat piece of granite makes a good bench, for instance, one to be placed under a wisteria pergola. Here it can be seen that the stone is not given a high polish, though wood is often varnished to bring out the beauty of its grain.*

carved into its sides, suggests a rustic well-head.

Just as the guests purify themselves with water, the host cleanses his garden with water before their arrival. The idea of purification takes its most stylized form in the "ornamental" privy found in the inner garden of the most traditional tea gardens. This is usually a simple room arranged with rocks and sand. It is not intended for use; like much else in the tea garden, the functional is turned into a work of art.

Nor is anything that looks ornamental actually superfluous. Tea gardens are intimate, not grand. They make a virtue of the tight, awkward spaces tucked around the side of buildings. Since modesty is considered a virtue in a host in Japan, the beauty of the tea garden comes from the cumulative effect of the simple and natural materials used for its fittings. Sen-no-Rikyu sought beauty in natural forms — for example, in the rocks he chose for his stepping-stones and basins. The three Sen schools of tea in Japan, each tracing its descent from one of Sen-no-Rikyu's grandsons, still faithfully preserve his tradition of the tea ceremony.

Another of Sen-no-Rikyu's own disciples took a different approach. Rather than trying to make gardens appear natural, Furuta Oribe (1543–1615) and his disciple, Kobori Enshu (1579–1647), sought to draw attention to their art. Oribe developed a style distinct from Rikyu's by deliberately introducing the artificial, the man-made, into his gardens. He set out to startle, to confound expectations, to draw attention to the artificiality of gardens. He defied convention by positioning his lanterns so that they tilted slightly, a hazardous thing to do in a country prone to earthquakes. He even transplanted towering dead trees into his gardens, and placed them so that they could not be ignored by his guests. He and Enshu both experimented with geometrical designs, using cut stone for paths instead

facing page: *Classic examples of tiny courtyard gardens are found in central Kyoto, where houses and shops jostle together along narrow, grid-like streets.*

Light filters down into this garden, which belongs to Ichi-riki-tei, an old tea-house restaurant. There is a well with a bamboo cover and a small shrine. The lanterns give a sense of shape to the yard. The planting is severely restricted to evergreens, which have a calming effect on the eye. The shape of each tree and shrub is very well defined.

of restricting themselves, like Rikyu, to naturally shaped stone. Even when it came to natural stone, Oribe sought out large rocks which split flawlessly along a seam so that they gave the impression of having been artificially cut. Whereas Rikyu had striven to exclude anything from the garden that attracted special attention to itself, Oribe and Enshu went so far as to emphasize design over function.

Characteristically, the Oribe school of tea came to be associated with a specific design of lantern

above: *This example of a traditional layout for a water basin is in Monaco. The basin is placed on a rock in the middle of a pebble-lined sink, or "ocean" as it is referred to in Japanese. The boulder to the right of the basin is intended to hold a basin of hot water. An added feeling of privacy is provided by the* koetsuji-*style sleeve fence.*

which still bears his name. While Oribe himself appears not to have restricted himself to any one design, his disciples eventually did, principally in order to establish their own individual style, distinguishing them from all the other various schools of tea, with which they were in hot competition for students and followers. Early tea masters had used discarded votive lanterns from old temples and shrines, but the *oribe* lantern did away with the base

and was intended to be stuck into the ground. It also departed from traditional styles in having a distinctive round bulge below the lantern cage. Many historians believe that the figure usually found carved on the shaft of early examples of this type of lantern came to be associated with Christ by Japanese converts to Christianity, and that these vaguely cross-shaped lanterns became their disguised objects of worship after Christianity was proscribed in 1612.

Strictly speaking, a *roji* is a tea garden only if it is intended for the use of the participants of a tea ceremony. Put another way, a garden is a tea garden no matter how simple it is, so long as it serves the functions of one, which is to prepare the guests for the ritual of tea-drinking. But even if you are not a tea master, the tea garden offers a distinct approach to the whole idea of gardening: rather than being a landscape to be admired, the tea garden can be appreciated only by walking through it a single step at a time – it is a series of constantly changing tableaux which cannot all be seen at once. It is also an enclosed space separated from the outside world by tall hedges, a traditional mud wall or a perimeter fence of closely-woven bamboo or of bamboo and cedar bark. In this sense, a tea garden condenses within a much smaller space the pleasures of a larger stroll garden. The difference is that the tea garden has a single purpose, which is to guide guests to a specific place. It is important that the expectations of your guests should not be disappointed, that the tea garden should lead somewhere special, whether it is a pergola, a gazebo or a summer-house.

Designing a tea garden

A point to keep in mind when designing a tea garden is that you do not want your guests to rush through it. The main gate into the garden needs to be carefully positioned, and plants strategically placed around it, so that the ultimate destination – the tea-house itself – is not in full view from the entrance. The garden should be allowed to unfold its own surprises. It is important, for example, that the bench in the outer garden should not allow guests a glimpse of their host bustling around with last-minute preparations in an adjoining area of the garden, for this would completely destroy any sense of occasion. A guest must not be harried into washing his or her hands by a conspicuously placed stone basin – it should be slightly hidden behind some greenery, or a short partition fence. A way of encouraging guests to take time in each part of the garden is to screen off parts of the next section. Many of the most celebrated tea gardens have more than one path, each leading into different areas of the garden, which are marked off by hedges or bamboo fences. The secret of designing a tea garden is to incorporate these features without creating a sense of clutter. The challenge is to make a small area seem more spacious than it really is.

Gravel, paths and plants

An important element in this is to discard the western idea of beds for shrubs and perennials. Areas within the garden can be distinguished not only by using fences and hedges, but also with gravel or ground-cover plants. Enshu created patterns in his gardens by covering wide sections of them with beautifully colored pebbles and leaving the rest bare and mossy. There he planted his few choice trees: *Prunus mume* (Japanese apricot), Japanese maples and pines. His stepping-stones boldly crossed both areas. Paths also have the effect of dividing a garden space into sections. The challenge is to integrate the paths into the overall design of the garden. A broad path can split a garden apart into halves; thus there has been a tendency to avoid them in many types of Japanese gardens, unless it is a path leading up to a formal gate. Stepping-stones, on the other hand, can help a

gravelly area to blend and merge seamlessly into an area devoted to moss. Ground-cover, moreover, does not have to consist of a single type of plant – this is not a lawn. It can be moss with tussocks of *Ophiopogon* or liriope, or it can be liriope varied with tufts of fern. This sort of mixed planting is more difficult if the predominant ground-cover is to be lawn grass.

Tea gardens are different from other types of Japanese gardens in that man-made hills, waterfalls and formally arranged groups of rocks do not play a

major role in them. Instead, it is the planting which determines the feel of the garden. Space being at a premium, the effect is produced not by a mass of closely planted vegetation, but by the shapes of carefully chosen specimen trees and bushes. Although shrubs like azaleas can be pruned into neat, round spheres, most plants are chosen for the gracefulness of their natural forms. Pruning is therefore more a question of tidying up – removing crossed, crowded

above: *This courtyard garden, belonging to the Ban family in central Kyoto, is planted in the manner of a tea garden. Horse-tail* (Equisetum hiemale) *forms a short screen around the water basin, while the scattered planting of Japanese maple, Japanese apricot and* Cleyera japonica *allows glimpses of a partly hidden stone lantern.*

or weak branches. The pleasures of Japanese gardens are those of Nature: her shapes, colors, and textures. Abstract shapes tend to be less important in a tea garden than in a Zen dry garden, where they might aid meditation. Oribe and Enshu, as we have seen, took a different approach. In the end, each school of tea has its own cherished traditions, but these precepts should guide, not stifle, the imagination.

Traditionally speaking, the most important thing when it comes to planting a tea garden is to meet the needs of the tea ceremony. The use of plants has always been an important way of controlling the amount of light which filters into the quiet preserve of the tea-room. Light that is too bright is considered distracting. It can be frankly uncomfortable. On the other hand, a room that is gloomy or damp can also be disagreeable. In countries where sunlight is weak during the winter months, it is probably a good idea to have deciduous trees near the room instead of the more traditional evergreens. This will let in whatever light is available. There has always been a tendency in Japan to prefer the privacy provided by evergreens, particularly conifers. This was Sen-no-Rikyu's own choice. He excluded everything in the garden which could distract attention away from the flower arranged in his tea-room. Rikyu is said to have dug up his entire patch of summer morning glories so that a single perfect bloom might be displayed for his patron Hideyoshi.

Oribe and Enshu introduced more diversity into the tea garden, although they too were sparing in the use of flowering and fruiting trees and shrubs. Even now, shrubs bearing small, pale flowers in shades of white or lavender are considered the most suitable for the subdued elegance of a tea garden: these include the more refined lace-cap hydrangeas and enkianthuses. Witch hazels have a pleasing tree shape and graceful yellow or orange ribbon-like flowers in late winter. Like any of the various Japanese maples available of differing leaf shapes and color, witch hazels can serve as a brilliant herald of the approach of autumn. Rikyu swept his tea gardens many hours before he expected his guests: any brightly colored leaves which fell afterwards he allowed to remain where they were on the moss. Oribe, on the other hand, chose only reddened dry pine needles to scatter under all his trees, whether they were conifers or not. Enshu went a step further and arranged the drifts of pine needles on his moss.

Flower petals – cherries, plum and camellias – are still often allowed to lie where they fall, since they scatter before they discolor, and they carpet the moss with their beautiful hues. However, cherries and camellias are not often planted in tea gardens as they are thought to be somewhat showy. It is also traditional to avoid shrubs which have stridently colored flowers, as well as unusual or curious plants which draw special attention to themselves. Also shunned are flowers like the gardenia, which have an overpowering scent. Since *roji* gardens tend to be narrow, any vigorous or bushy plants will cause problems by quickly overgrowing their allotted space. It is therefore advisable to keep branches trimmed and out of the way of the path. Moss is often grown between stepping stones so that guests will not slip on wet leaves or grass.

If space is very limited, a sense of openness can be created by reducing the amount of underplanting, and choosing short ground-covering plants like moss and *Ophiopogon* to go under the specimen trees. Hostas, *Farfugium japonicum* and *Aspidistra elatior*, with their architectural leaves, can look striking if they are not overcrowded and swamped by other plants. Treat them, as well as shrubs such as *Daphniphyllum macropodum* and *Dendropanax trifidus*, as you would specimen trees: allow each plant just enough space for it to be admired properly. In order to emphasize the height of larger trees, the lower branches should be removed.

Naturally, there will be appropriate places for visitors to pause as they walk along the path – where there is a gate, for instance, or a bench, or a fork in the path, marked by a stepping-stone larger than the rest. Other significant spots around the garden include stone basins and the actual door of the tea-house from which your guest will go back into the garden. All of these will be the principal vantage-points from which the garden will be seen. Position the most important garden features with this in mind. A specimen tree, such as *Torreya nucifera* (Japanese nutmeg yew), *Ilex integra*, *Ternstroemia gymnanthera* or *Ginkgo biloba* (maidenhair tree), is sometimes planted near the gate for the guests to admire as they leave the garden. Another tradition has been to plant a large pine behind the tea-house so it can be seen above the roofline and add depth to the garden.

Plants for a tea garden

Hedging: *Cleyera japonica, Eurya japonica.*

Flowering shrubs: *Enkianthus perulatus, Hydrangea paniculata, Rhaphiolepis umbellata, Rhododendron quinquefolium, Styrax japonicum.*

Around a basin: *Nandina domestica* (heavenly bamboo), *Pieris japonica* (Japanese andromeda), *Eurya japonica, Aucuba japonica* (spotted laurel), ferns, *Equisetum hiemale* (scouring rush, horsetail).

Behind or near stone lanterns: pruned pines, *Castanopsis cuspidata, Ilex crenata* (box-leaved holly), *I. integra, Sorbus commixta* (Japanese rowan), *Ternstroemeria gymnanthera, Torreya nucifera* (Japanese nutmeg yew).

"Wild" flowers: *Saxifraga stolonifera, Disporum smilacinum, Polygonatum falcatum* (fragrant Solomon's seal), *Platycodon grandiflorum* (balloon flower), *Tricyrtis hirta* (toad lily).

facing page: *This water basin, situated in a public, open area of the Japanese Garden near Portland, Oregon, does not have the customary group of rocks surrounding it. The pruned mugo pine to the right and a slightly shorter Japanese maple to the left provide a feeling of height to the overall arrangement and, along with the neatly clipped hedge and the large rock in the foreground, subtly produce a sense of place.*

The courtyard garden

The hill and pond garden, the dry garden and the tea garden are the three historical branches of the Japanese tradition in gardening. However, in practical terms, the buildings – the merchants' and artisans' houses, the shops, inns and restaurants – that formed the heart of the ancient city of Kyoto, that epicenter of the art of Japanese gardening, were, and still are, very cramped for space. With perhaps only a room or two facing onto the street, these buildings are narrow and long. And as you pass along their maze-like succession of rooms, you will come across tiny, square, courtyard gardens, wells of greenery surrounded on all sides by rooms and corridors.

The smallest of these courtyard gardens are called *tsubo-niwa*, a *tsubo* being the basic square measure used in Japan for calculating space – it equals 36 ft^2 (3.3 m^2). These gardens are very private, meant to be seen up close, often in passing, as people move from one room to another.

If the garden is open on all sides to various rooms and corridors, it needs to be designed so it can be appreciated from all angles. It will also tend to be quite shady. In the built-up areas of Kyoto, not much light manages to find its way into many of these minuscule gardens, though they are open to the elements and catch the rain. These gardens are often ideal for that beloved component of all Japanese gardens, moss. Where moss refuses to oblige and thrive, *Ophiopogon* can be used instead for ground-cover. Other shade-tolerant plants, like *Aucuba japonica* (spotted laurel) and *Fatsia japonica*, are chosen to complement perhaps a moss-grown stone lantern or a stone basin. These would not be meant for actual use, although a lantern could be lit sometimes, and usually several handsome stepping-stones will also be laid across the tiny space. Admittedly, these gardens can look somewhat somber, particularly if they are planted with evergreens. Yet that slightly musty smell of leaf-mould that blends so naturally with the scent of the wood of which traditional houses were built characterizes Japan. Modern commercial and municipal buildings which employ a lot of glass often manage to produce a more airy feeling to their courtyard gardens than the wood, wattle and daub, and tiled-roof construction of traditional Japanese city dwellings. One way to brighten an enclosed courtyard garden is to use fine gravel to create, if not a completely dry garden with groups of rocks, a simple garden with bamboo, for instance. The fine gravel can be raked into patterns. The Imperial

Palace at Kyoto has gardens of this kind, laid out with clean white gravel, in each of which only one kind of shrub is grown: wisteria, bamboo, or Japanese bush clover.

When designing a tiny courtyard garden, as with any other kind of garden, it is necessary to keep in mind how and from where it is to be seen. Remember that in all probability the viewer will be standing. Since Japanese houses are always raised above ground level, a tall rock may not seem as impressive seen from this height as it would be from a sitting position on a verandah. On the other hand, if a tiny garden is to be viewed from a standing position, a very flat stone can be effective against a background of white gravel. A very low ground-cover plant like *Liriope muscari*, with its elegant leaves and pale flower spikes, can appear insignificant if it can only be seen from above and from a great height. Partition fences woven of bamboo, or using other kinds of grasses or even bark, can be used to separate off areas even in the smallest gardens. These sleeve fences do not extend all the way across the garden,

above: *Decking here creates a raised corridor from which the courtyard garden can be viewed. The corridor allows a close-up view of the fine* Pieris japonica *and the bronze-leafed maple. The shallow end of the pool is laid with pebbles, and the planting, consisting of marginals such as rushes and water irises, is arranged in groups among the rocks to provide areas of clear water on which the maple can cast its reflection.*

but serve as a sort of rustic screen. For instance, they help to make a doorway more sheltered, and they add to the tiniest gardens that element of partial concealment and surprise which has always been important in Japanese garden design.

Trees with a gracefully branching habit, like maples and witch hazels, will draw attention to the horizontal. They can be planted for contrast next to a slender tree such as a small, carefully pruned pine-tree. Tall, slender plants like bamboos and pines will emphasize height, especially if their lower branches are meticulously removed and they are not cluttered with underplanting. The juxtaposition of the tall with the short will create a sense of spaciousness even in small gardens.

A shade-tolerant daphne, like *Daphne odora*, will turn a tiny courtyard garden into a well of scent in early spring. Japanese gardens do not have an off-season, for they are on show all year round. This is why evergreens play such an important role. Green is undoubtedly the dominant color of Japanese gardens. The pleasure of winter comes from waking to find frost patterns on the leaves of *Aucuba japonica* (spotted laurel), or a mound of snow perched on a stone lantern. This will give some idea of the importance of the initial choice and layout of the various components of the garden. Herbaceous plants do not substantially change the look and feel of traditional Japanese gardens during the spring and summer months as they do in western gardens with mixed borders and beds. Plants need to be chosen for their year-round interest – for the shape of their individual leaves, for the gracefulness of their branches and for their overall shape. This is especially the case in an intimate enclosed garden. It would be sad if such a garden was allowed to fall into neglect; it would be a constant reminder and reproach – an embarrassing, cluttered cupboard that is always open.

The courtyard garden can look back to any of

facing page: A lantern is sometimes placed on the far shore of a pond or lake to focus the eye. Larger ponds demand a tall kasuga *lantern rather than this smaller* oribe *lantern, which is right for this intimate courtyard garden designed by Paul Fleming.*

In place of a lantern, an expansive hill-and-lake stroll garden might have a group of rocks representing a waterfall.

above: *This is an example of a tall stone water basin, intended for use from the verandah if the room for the tea ceremony was located in the house. Horsetail (*Equisetum hiemale*) is very popular in Japan for planting around water basins.*

This arrangement is by Marc Peter Keane, the American garden designer and writer who lives and works in Kyoto.

the other traditional types of gardens. Moss and white gravel can be arranged to represent an island in the ocean. The moss can surround a rock or a choice shrub. The gardener might decide to model a courtyard garden on the most austere and abstract Zen garden, with sand and rocks and no plants. A bed of pebbles can be made to represent a meandering stream, with a miniature stone lantern indicating a headland jutting out into symbolic water. A lantern

left: *This garden by Marc Peter Keane incorporates a western-style patio and water feature. The eaves of the house extend out to form a pergola, up which vines have been planted. Akebia quinata and Stauntonia hexaphylla are both fruiting climbers used for pergolas. The leaning tree in the foreground is supported in the traditional Japanese manner against a horizontal piece of timber.*

above: *The slender trunks of these maples become a feature of this courtyard garden in their own right. The eye is drawn to the verdure of the underplanting: the soft mosses, the leathery aspidistra, and the delicate fronds of the ferns. In the middle of the garden water trickles from a bamboo spout into a small pool, suggesting a natural spring. This garden was designed by Paul Sheppard.*

next to a stone basin refers back to the graceful hospitality of the tea garden.

This is the most flexible type of garden, which does not have to be restricted to inner courtyards of old houses. Miniature gardens of this kind can make use of any confined or awkward strip of garden around the house. The smallest and narrowest

low, open-weave bamboo fence. The outer area of the garden can be used to indulge a passion for a wide range of plants. The inner garden then becomes the sanctum, an uncluttered refuge with a stone lantern and a basin, or a haven with a single pool of water. It will thus become a restful place of reflection, contemplation and peace.

facing page: *A glass roof lets plenty of bright Australian sunlight into this pond garden in Melbourne. The island in the center of the pond is connected by a stone-slab bridge to the Japanese-style verandah.*

garden can be created in the space available outside a ground-floor window. It can be embellished with a lantern, a basin, or a rock, with raked white gravel, *Ophiopogon*, or a single specimen of *Nandina domestica* (heavenly bamboo). One way of utilizing a long and narrow urban back garden surrounded by high fencing or walls is to make a virtue of the sense of privacy it already possesses. The garden can be divided into two parts, informally indicated by a

Plants

As in tea gardens, it is a good idea in warm climates to give this type of garden a good sprinkling of water before the arrival of guests so that the plants and rocks do not look hot and dusty but cool, fresh and gently inviting.

Bamboo canes that are more than two or three years old should be cut back to ground level. New shoots will then emerge in the spring, or in the

above: *A yukimi-style lantern is commonly used alongside water as in this Californian courtyard garden.*

left: *A gateway opens into a courtyard dominated by a monolithic rock feature with a cascade. The sliding glass doors with which the courtyard is surrounded help to keep this garden bright and prevent the central feature from becoming too oppressive. More time is needed for the planting to grow into the right shapes and sizes to become an integral part of the design.*

autumn, in the case of winter-shooting varieties of the *Chimonobambusa* group. Bamboos should be transplanted about a month before the shoots are expected. Do not let the roots dry out while transplanting them. Bamboo is often planted in groups of three, five or seven, since these are considered to be auspicious numbers in Japan.

Bamboos are not usually combined with showy flowering shrubs. They do go well with *Iris japonica* and ferns, including *Matteuccia struthiopteris* (ostrich fern). Other plants often used for underplanting bamboo include *Ardisia crispa, A. japonica, Pachysandra terminalis* (Japanese spurge), and *Calanthe discolor.*

Traditional plants for the courtyard garden

Specimen plants: *Musa basjoo* (Japanese banana), *Cycas revoluta* (Japanese sago palm), *Fatsia japonica.*

For underplanting: *Iris japonica, Liriope muscari, Ophiopogon japonicus.*

For ground-cover: *Ophiopogon japonicus, Sasa* spp., *Ardisia japonica.*

"Wild" flowers near a plant-pot: *Equisetum hiemale* (horsetail), *Ardisia japonica, Saxifraga stolonifera, Rohdea japonica.*

For a dry rock garden: *Hepatica* spp., *Matteuccia struthiopteris* (ostrich fern), gentians, *Selaginella tamariscina, Rohdea japonica, Platycodon grandiflorum* (balloon flower), *Reineckea carnea, Ajuga nipponensis* (Japanese bugle), *Bletilla striata, Tricyrtis hirta* (toad lily), *Ardisia japonica, Commelina communis, Aquilegia* spp. (columbines), *Physalis alkekengi* (Chinese lantern), *Eupatorium japonicum.*

CHAPTER TWO

The Elements of a Japanese Garden

The features that go into the composition of a Japanese garden all have their part to play in the creation of a single serene and harmonious landscape. Although western eyes may at first be confounded by the formality of the pruning and the abstraction of the groupings of rocks, the Japanese have always characterized their various garden styles as naturalistic, for each in its own way seeks to represent a vision of Nature that is calming, contemplative and beautiful.

Plants

There is at least one subtle difference between western gardens and traditional Japanese ones; though it is not often pointed out, it is absolutely fundamental. The Japanese do not confine shrubs and perennials to beds. You will not find that familiar feature of western gardens – the contrast between the open, even sweep of a well-manicured lawn and the riot of colors and textures confined to herbaceous borders and beds. Japanese gardens contrive to create an impression of luxuriance without actually using a great many plants. Individual trees or shrubs are carefully positioned so that they suggest the presence of a whole thicket, or even a forest. Each plant is chosen for its shape. Pruning therefore becomes a very important task, the principle being to bring out the inherent shapeliness of the plant by careful trimming and removing awkwardly placed, overcrowded branches.

For all shrubs and trees, it is important to clear away weak or dead wood and remove congested branches, downward-pointing growth and long, non-flowering spurs. Suckers, which sap energy from the plant and may also be growing from the root-stock if the plant has been grafted, should also be cut out.

Shaping plants

Perhaps shrubs and trees are trained and pruned harder in Japan than western taste allows. None the less, pruned plants play an important part in the overall design, for their sinuous outlines give rhythm and movement to the Japanese garden.

The basic idea is to observe and respect the

inherent shape of a plant. Many trees helpfully give us clues to the shapes hidden within them. There are conical conifers such the sawara cypress, *Sciadopitys verticillata* (Japanese umbrella pine) and *Juniperus chinensis* "Kaizuka". Trees of this type need hardly any pruning at all to keep their shape. *Dendropanax trifidus* and *Daphniphyllum macropodum*, both of them good evergreens, are likewise popular for their fine shapes. Japanese maples, witch hazels and deciduous azaleas, such as *Rhododendron quinquefolium*, *R. reticulatum* and *R. japonicum*, have naturally delicate, branching forms; *Camellia sasanqua*, *Stewartia pseudocamellia* and the smaller *S. monadelpha* grow into columns without any help. All dislike being pruned, and require only the minimum degree of maintenance, like all trees and shrubs, which is to have dead, weak or diseased

right: *The shape of this neatly clipped pine, more commonly used for box-leaved holly, shows off one of the most popular subjects for topiary in Japan. This pine is in Mrs Pomeroy's Californian garden.*

previous page: *A sudden spell of cold weather late in the autumn produces the best color in Japanese maples, which can be breathtaking. One of the most reliable and popular of the autumnal red-leaved maples is "Osakazuki" (Moon of Osaka). Let the leaves rest for a while where they have fallen, for they produce drifts of color on the ground. Flowering Japanese cherries shed their petals in a similarly decorative way.*

branches cleared away to allow new growth.

When buying trees and shrubs, it is important to look for young plants which have the potential to grow into the shapes needed in the garden. For example, a *Daphne odora* sapling which is already leggy will be difficult to prune into a globe. Some *Ilex integra*, *Osmanthus heterophyllus* (Chinese holly) and yew saplings will be suitable for growing into bushy domes; other young plants of the same species may

have strong central trunks, which will make them good subjects for more elaborate topiary.

Ilex crenata (box-leaved holly), *Podocarpus macrophyllus* (yew pine) and *Ternstroemia gymnanthera* can all be trimmed into beautiful domes. So can garden camellias. *Ilex crenata* is also a good hedging plant, along with *Taxus cuspidata* var. *nana* (dwarf yew) and semi-evergreen azaleas. These low-growing shrubs are often clipped into neat globes, and are important in

above: *This bonsai pine tree has been trained in such a way as to emphasize one long side branch, supported by a stout bamboo cane. Taller trees are often trained so that a long branch extends over a pond or a lake. Even taller pines are trained so a branch stretches over a gate or along the front of a building.*

Japanese topiary

1 *Bamboos grown in the garden often have their lower branches removed to emphasize height. When they are evenly dotted around a garden, they form a cool canopy of leaves. Sinobambusa tootsik is a popular choice in Japan for this treatment. Specimen bamboos grown in large plant pots can retain some of their lower branches, but they should be evenly spaced along the central stem.*

2 *A curved trunk on pines is made by supporting the tree with stout bamboo canes, which are also used to train large branches on pines, yews, and box-leaved holly. To create an open tree shape, branches are pulled downwards and fastened with rope to the tree trunk. Any stems growing along the underside of the branches are removed so that all the growth sits on top of the branches in a rounded mound.*

3 *A tiered shape is ideal for* Ternstroemia gymnanthera. *It is also used for* Cryptomeria japonica.

4 *Enkianthuses and taller semi-evergreen azaleas may eventually lose most of their leaves towards the base. Clear away small twigs and weak growth from the lower parts of the main branches. The leafy top can be trimmed round or into a fan shape. The latter also suits some of the shorter varieties of Japanese maples.*

5 *A pine tree can be trained to stretch a branch over a gateway. This type of topiary is suitable for the most formal areas around a house, usually by the front gate.*

6: *Some trees, such as the Japanese yew (*Taxus cuspidata*), Podocarpus* macrophyllus *and some Japanese maples and oaks, produce straight, upright* branches from the trunk. As with pine trees, any stems growing sideways or downwards are removed in order to create neat, rounded clusters at the ends of the branches.

left: *Pruned conifers, like this juniper, look particularly handsome against a white garden wall.* Juniperus chinensis *is traditionally pruned by pinching off the tender tips by hand; this is done to order to prevent die-back. This example is situated in Mrs Pomeroy's garden in California.*

right: *Pine trees can be restricted in height to suit the size of a garden. This photograph shows how good pruning has encouraged all the fine branches to grow upwards, producing the characteristic bun-shaped clusters of healthy needles. These established pines no longer need to have their main branches supported with bamboo canes.*

left: *The bamboo canes and dyed black hemp rope used to train this Japanese white pine have become decorative features in their own right.*

right: Ternstroemia gymnanthera *used to be indispensable in Japanese gardens. This example, from Ritsurin Park in Takamatsu, is pruned in the traditional way with the number of side branches radically reduced to give the tree an airy look. The bamboo fence in the foreground is in the yotsume style. It is also often constructed using groups of two vertical canes instead of one.*

Japanese gardens as they are thought to "anchor" a group of taller, more slender trees. They are often placed in the garden to suggest well-weathered, well-rounded rocks, which themselves symbolize Nature's timelessness, age and harmony.

Of all the shapes found in Japanese gardens, the most striking must be the clipped pines and yews which are made to look like giant bonsai. In the West,

snow. The undersides of the branches are cleared of needles, so that the flowing lines of the trunk and the branches are clearly visible — hence the Japanese enthusiasm for the Yoshino cherry, whose immense clusters of snowy pink blossoms seem to float like clouds above leafless, black, arching branches. *Ilex integra, Ternstroemia gymnanthera, Osmanthus heterophyllus* (Chinese holly) and *Thujopsis dolabrata* (hiba arborvitae), all of which have an upright habit, also take well to this kind of pruning. The ideal season for this operation is mid-summer. Capillary roots are severed by making a wide circle around the tree with a clean spade. At the same time, most of the side branches along the straight central trunk (which can be reduced if the tree is too tall) are removed, except for a number of strong, healthy, well-placed ones. These are pruned back to within 2 to 3 ft (60 to 90 cm) of the trunk, the aim being to encourage new bushy growth at the tip of each of them. Open wounds on the tree are protected with an anti-fungal preparation and wax. After the new growth has been left to develop for about three years, it is clipped round neatly every summer. This type of topiary is often used on vigorous trees which have outgrown their allotted space in the garden.

in the nineteenth century, opinion was divided between those who dismissed them as grotesque and those who found the shapes bizarre but were at least prepared to acknowledge the skill involved in training them. Even today, in spite of changing fashions in Japan, these elaborately trained evergreens are still found in domestic gardens as well as in distinguished temple parks.

On each of a pine's severely reduced number of branches, the needles nestle like mounds of moist

Ilex crenata (box-leaved holly), *Podocarpus macrophylla* (yew pine) and *Taxus cuspidata* var. *nana* (dwarf yew) are also suitable for this treatment. Because they are pliant, it may be preferable to use on them a technique which is used for pines, where the trunks are trained to curve in a sinuous line. It is true that in Japan this kind of topiary is an art practised by professional gardeners, but there is nothing to stop an adventurous amateur from giving it a try.

A tree will begin to take shape after about five years, but it will take as much as fifteen to twenty years for it to mature into its final form. The subject should already have reached the desired height and size before it is trained. It should have been planted

72

facing page, above: *Another border at Ryoan-ji is planted with trees but not in order of their height. A woodland effect is produced by restricting the number of plants and meticulously refining their shapes. Shrubs such as* Euonymus japonicus *scattered among the trees help to fill empty spaces without distracting the eye.*

facing page, below: *Tall trees with slender trunks are not considered as obstacles to a view. On the contrary, they help to frame a landscape. Here* hinoki *cypresses (*Chamaecyparis obtusa*), with their lovely red pillar-like trunks, serve this purpose. The trees have been planted at equal intervals.*

in its final site for at least a year, preferably at an angle to the ground which makes shaping the trunk somewhat easier. The primary curve should be in the bottom half of the tree. Support the upper part of the curved trunk with a sturdy cane, and use another to hold this support in place. A good, sturdy branch should grow outwards from the arc formed by the trunk. This branch should be allowed to grow longer than the rest of the side branches. There should also be another, shorter side branch growing in the opposite direction lower down the trunk; this serves to counterbalance the tree's longest branch. The overall number of branches should be reduced so that the ones remaining are more or less evenly spaced along the central trunk and point in all directions around the tree. Gently bend them downwards for a more open shape, and support them with bamboo, securing these canes in turn to the trunk with rope. Prune away all the twigs on the underside of the branches. The work should be carried out between late winter and early spring, and in the case of pines it should be undertaken before the new buds begin to break.

The point of this kind of Japanese topiary is to create a sense of balance through asymmetry. It involves finding a balance between the vertical pull of the trunk and the horizontal line of the branches. There are many uses for this kind of topiary in Japanese gardens. A single specimen pine (either the Japanese black or red pine) is often grown at an angle next to the main garden gate, and trained so that one of its branches extends over it like an arch. Pines are also trained to hang over ponds and lakes, so that the reflection of their branches in the water can be enjoyed by the visitor.

It will come as no surprise that pines are meticulously pruned to preserve their elegant shape. The process has two stages. In the middle of spring, the number of new buds is reduced to two or three on each branch. Those which are either weak or too vigorous should be pinched off: in the case of *Pinus densiflora* (Japanese red pine) and *P. parviflora* (Japanese white pine), the size of the remaining buds should be reduced by a quarter to a third, while *P. thunbergii* (Japanese black pine) can have its buds reduced by a half or more. In the autumn, the tree is stripped of its old needles by rubbing each branch gently between the hands from its base towards its tip. The needles growing on the last 3 in (7 cm) or so at the end of each branch are left, for this should be the current year's growth. This procedure is particularly necessary if the buds have not been trimmed back in the spring. Less drastic grooming will be sufficient if greater growth is desired.

Arranging trees and shrubs

Topiary yews in the shape of globes, pyramids and obelisks helped to emphasize the symmetrical harmony of the gardens of the great French seventeenth-century chateaux of Vaux-le-Vicomte and Versailles. Japanese gardening, in contrast, seeks harmony in asymmetry. We have seen this in the design of topiary, and the same applies to the arrangement of trees and shrubs. Instead of working with even numbers of plants, Japanese gardeners think in odd numbers. The basic unit is three trees or shrubs, which can be augmented with a further pair of plants to bring the total to five. An arrangement of seven plants can similarly be broken down into groups of five and two. Nine plants can be thought of as three groups of three, and so on.

The principal trio should be of different heights, shapes and textures so as to give a pleasant diversity to the grouping. Juxtaposing deciduous trees or shrubs with evergreens ensures interest all the year round. Begin by choosing the tree that will form the central focus of the entire planting scheme. Allow its habit to suggest which trees or shrubs might go well

with it. These should help to counterbalance any
peculiar characteristics the principal tree might have –
perhaps the way it leans in a certain direction or the
general shape formed by its branches. The shortest
plant in the group will usually serve to anchor the
whole arrangement.

A classical combination is a conifer, such as a pine
or an *Ilex crenata* (box-leaved holly), with a Japanese
maple, adding a bushy, shorter evergreen, such as
Citrus tachibana or *Cleyera japonica*, to give stability to the
group. Pines and maples could also be planted beside
a deciduous shrub, such as *Corylopsis pauciflora*, to let
more light into the garden. A tall, fully grown
camellia would also serve admirably as the focus of a
group, combined, for example, with an evergreen such
as *Ilex crenata* (box-leaved holly), clipped into a globe,
and the softer green of a satsuki azalea. Azaleas are
perhaps the most versatile plants in the Japanese
garden. Not only can they be pruned singly, they
can also be treated together to form a broad swathe
or a low, narrow hedge to mark or separate distinct
areas within the garden. Popular plants such as
maples, satsuki azaleas and *Pieris japonica* (Japanese
andromeda) are reliable companions for space-
filling evergreens such as *Ternstroemia gymnanthera* or
Daphniphyllum macropodum.

In order to give the illusion of depth to a group
of trees and shrubs, the three plants should be laid
out so that their bases form a scalene triangle, that is,
one with sides of unequal lengths. Since the plants
will be of different heights, none of them should be
completely hidden from view. To this end, place them
so that once they have reached their desired size
(about three years after planting), they form a triangle
when seen from the primary vantage-points around
the garden.

The scalene triangle is also the basic figure to
keep in mind when combining groups of plants. In a
plant arrangement of this kind, always think of the

central tree in each group as one of the points of the triangle.

When it comes to the choice of trees and shrubs, there is no hard and fast rule about what goes with

number of different kinds of plants used in a single garden. Conifers and evergreens provide a background tapestry of green, against which each of the seasons can be evoked by a splash of color provided by one or

above: *One of the largest stroll gardens in Japan, found at Shugakuin Imperial Palace, was constructed in the middle of the seventeenth century.*

what. Many of the best-loved Japanese plants, such as azaleas, camellias and Japanese maples, are acid-loving. If your garden is very alkaline, it may be safer to grow these plants in pots, bearing in mind that they will need rainwater rather than the kind supplied by the local water board which is likely to contain all manner of chemicals.

There is a tendency in Japan to restrict the

two appropriate plants: witch hazels, camellias or daphnes in late winter, enkianthuses, wisterias and azaleas in spring, *Cornus kousa*, crape myrtle and *Stewartia pseudocamellia* in summer, maples in autumn, *Ardisia crispa* with its red berries in winter. In large gardens, a clump of tall, columnar conifers, such as firs, can be planted to set off shorter, more rounded evergreens and deciduous trees.

Rocks

The importance of rocks in Japanese gardens cannot be overestimated, for the veneration of sacred rocks goes back to the earliest times. Rocks for the garden are chosen on the basis of their color, their grain and the way they have been worn by the elements. Whether they have been scarred by volcanic activity or polished smooth by the ceaseless motion of waves, their attractiveness is thought to depend greatly on their power to evoke images and reflections. Rocks are set in Japanese gardens with the same view to the future with which trees were planted in the great English landscape gardens of the eighteenth century; the gardener looks to the future, to a time when the rocks will have been all but buried in moss.

right: *It is quite a challenge to make groups of big rocks look right in a garden, for the aim is to make them appear as though they belong naturally in their setting. The best way of doing this is always to bury the base of rocks in the ground. This cluster of rocks is set halfway down a slope to create an illusion that they have tumbled down there.*

previous page: *The tea-house in the Japanese Garden at Tatton Park in Cheshire stands on a small island surrounded by streams and a tiny water garden. Mounds of earth have been built on the island to vary the terrain and the whole island is covered in moss. The tea-house is shaded by several brilliantly colored Japanese maples, like the one shown here.*

Shapes and types of rock

There are several basic classifications of rock shapes, and each has its uses. The most important shape is that of the tall standing rock. Others include broad horizontal rocks (which may be more or less flat, uneven or step-shaped on top), very low flat rocks, round rocks, rocks in the shape of a low mound and rocks that lean diagonally. The last two are particularly useful for suggesting some of the geological changes the earth has undergone. A low, smooth, mound-like rock can make us think of the power of erosion, while a sharply slanting rock can look as though it has just been thrust up from the depths of the earth.

Since Japan is made up of a chain of volcanic islands, the kind of rock most commonly found is volcanic: andesite, granite, chlorite and basalt. Tufa is also found. Rock is also classified according to its terrain — mountain, river, valley or sea coast — for rocks will have weathered in different ways depending on where they have been collected.

Choosing rocks

Just as there are stringent regulations all over the world on taking plants or animals from the wild, inanimate objects like rocks must likewise not be removed from their natural environment. They must always be obtained from an approved source. All over Japan there are now strict controls regarding river stone, for which there is still a great demand for both gardening and building. Since the Japanese have always valued naturally shaped stone over quarried stone, this poses a serious problem if there is no standard way of acquiring the former. In some places

it may be possible to obtain rock that has been cleared from land intended for new fields or buildings. Otherwise, look for local quarries and take advice from local Japanese garden societies. It is a question of making the best use of locally available material, even though it may have been intended for a different purpose – for alpine rockeries, for example, or dry-stone walls.

Try to choose rocks which do not have a square-cut appearance that makes them look like rejected building material. Avoid sharp edges and right angles; they make the rock look plain and rough at the same time. Energy and movement on the one hand, and refinement, elegance and mellowness on the other are all desirable qualities. Look for interesting contours, surfaces and colors; clearly marked strata, for example, give a sense of history and the passage of time. Tufa, a porous rock found with mineral

above: *This Japanese domestic garden is designed in the manner of a flat sand Zen garden. The three groups of rocks are laid out in the form of a scalene triangle. The massive triangular rock left of center represents both a sacred mountain and a wing of a crane, and the flat stone bridge on the right is also a turtle's shell.*

facing page: *Japanese gardens strive for a sense of harmony with Nature by trying to integrate the man-made with what is natural. In this garden by Terry Welch, the wooden planks used for the gate blend beautifully with the landscape of native conifers, while the contrast between the natural grace of the firs and the refined beauty of the pruned pines draws attention to the powers and limitations of human creativity.*

Herbaceous plants, such as tall Japanese anemones (perhaps the white single "Honorine Jobert", "Géant des Blanches", or the pink "Max Vogel") can be used in a garden of this type.

deposits, has a unique texture and surface, but it has also been popular in the West for centuries, and supplies are diminishing. Many limestone areas are perilously close to disappearing altogether, for which reason limestone must not be used unless it is definitely known to be second-hand stone quarried a long time ago. Weathered, second-hand slate is also available sometimes.

Arranging rocks

It is important that rocks should be laid so they look as if they belong naturally into the landscape. For example, they are much more interesting when they give the illusion of being the tip of something vast lying hidden underground. Thus they are often set so that the rock seems to emerge from the ground at its broadest part. A rock that swells gently out of the ground reproduces the archetypal, maternal shape of Japanese mountains. Rocks that look precarious are frowned upon. They should never be set in such a

way that they taper towards ground level.

If a particular rock has blemishes, sharp corners or a bad shape, it may be possible to disguise its imperfections by using it in combination with other rocks or with low, ground-hugging shrubs. However, rocks will always have more of an impact if there are not too many of them cluttering an area. Go for fewer, larger rocks rather than an array of smaller pieces. An alternative is to work out an arrangement in which only the attractive parts of the rocks emerge above ground level. A single rock can be incorporated into the top of a man-made mound so that the only visible part of its surface, peering out of the moss, can seems like the bare face of a miniature mountain. It is also important to remember that newly planted shrubs and trees will eventually grow and make those precious rocks look smaller than they did when everything was first laid out. Although a newly planted garden will inevitably look bare, it is important to try to anticipate how the mature plants

Arranging groups of stones

1: *The base of a rock should always be set in the ground so that the visible part of it looks broader nearer the gound (a). It should never taper towards the ground (b).*

2: *The basic group of three rocks should be arranged so that they form a scalene triangle when seen from the side.*

3:. *The shape of the biggest and central stone of any group determines the feel of the landscape they create. A tall, rough, upright*

stone suggests a craggy mountain landscape, while a smooth, low stone resembles an ancient, eroded hill in miniature.

4: *A group of three rocks should be laid out so that their highest points form a rough scalene triangle when seen from above. The idea of the scalene triangle is not a fixed rule, but a useful tool to use when considering how far apart and in what sort of relation to each other the stones should be arranged.*

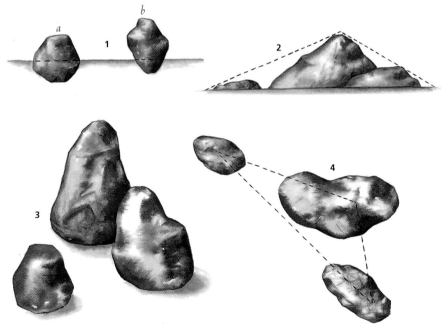

will eventually balance the groups of rocks and any other inanimate features you might wish to include, such as stone lanterns and fences.

Often a single, imposing rock gives an austere dignity to a garden, particularly at the front of a house. It can stand alone in gravel, or it can be embellished with low shrubs or a small tree, such as a Japanese maple. On the other hand, it can be surrounded by elegant tall canes of bamboo which have been carefully stripped of their lower branches. A rock of this kind, as well as tilted stones, must be carefully set and braced underground with more stones, so that they are absolutely secure and cannot topple over.

Combinations of more than two rocks should be of the same material, even if their size and shape are different. The idea is that they should look as if they all belong together. The basic unit is once again the group of three, in the shape of a scalene triangle. Show off the main rock of the group to its best advantage. Like human faces, rocks have their best sides, although some ruggedness may be attractive in either. The oldest advice on arranging stones comes to us from the eleventh century: give a rock what it cries out for. Give it what it needs to make it look secure and stable. Any additional stones are there to complement the principal piece. Japanese gardens have always sought to create a sense of balance and harmony out of what appears to be asymmetrical. Avoid setting out the rocks in a row or at right angles to each other. The whole group should look stable and solid together; the rocks should not look as though they are precariously propping each other up. Around the main group of three, an arrangement can be expanded to include ultimately five, seven or even fifteen stones.

The principal rock should be set so that its face is turned slightly sideways when seen from the front. Another point to keep in mind is that in a stroll garden a group of rocks should be interesting when seen from different angles. One trick to give added depth to your garden is to place larger rocks in the foreground and smaller ones in the distance, so they look further away than they really are. The same strategy can be applied to the placing of trees, where delicately branched trees are deliberately planted in the distance. A solid stone which seems to reach up to the sky imparts a sense of calm dignity and adds gravitas to a garden. Many rocks, on the other hand, leaning towards one side or another, draw the eye in a particular direction. Groups of rocks can exploit this to help create the dynamics of the garden, and their shapes can determine the principal direction in which the eye of the viewer is led through the composition of the garden.

Home-grown religious associations, with which rocks were always imbued, were reinforced by various Chinese religious traditions which, along with Buddhism, began to cross the Sea of Japan in the fourth and fifth centuries. Buddhist mythology included several holy mountains, while the Chinese possessed their own myth of a Mountain Isle of Eternal Youth (Mount Horai in Japanese) which was thought to be inhabited by immortal wise men. By the eleventh century, when rocks became an integral part of Japanese gardening styles, they were already being associated with these sacred places.

Buddhist mountains

There are two important mountains in the Buddhist tradition in Japan. One is Mount Fudaraku, considered to be the home of Kannon, the goddess of mercy. A single massive rock often has the double function of conveying an image of this fabled mountain to the initiate, while at the same time tapping more indigenous religious sentiments. The other mountain belonging to Buddhist lore is

Shumisen, the mountain at the center of the universe. Surrounded by seven seas, encircled in turn by seven golden mountains, an ocean, and finally a ring of iron mountains, Shumisen inspired cluster formations of rocks.

Apart from these specific references, the Buddhist tradition of portraying various Buddhas in groups of three gives an added religious dimension to the basic group of three rocks. These arrangements are called *sanzonseki*, which can be translated as "stones suggesting three Buddhas". The old gardening masters, however, were superstitious about placing a three-Buddha stone group in the center of the main view from the house. Not only did it suggest to them the imminence of death,

but it offended their sense of the rightness of asymmetry. For this reason, important features in the garden were invariably placed slightly to the left or slightly to the right of the central line of vision.

Zen gardens sometimes include a big flat-topped rock on which a monk could practise *zazen*, or meditation. Sometimes in a dry garden a boat-shaped rock can be found floating on an ocean of sand. This represents a celestial boat which, according to Japanese mythology, descended to earth from the skies in the time of the gods. There is also a Chinese tradition of a heavenly boat which carries in it the seven gods of good fortune.

Representations of Mount Horai, the Chinese Island of Eternal Youth, can be distinguished from

above: *A raised pathway acts as a stage of which the centerpiece is this simple but powerful combination of conifers and rocks, designed by Peter Chan and Brenda Sacoor. The rocks, with their bases securely planted in the ground, look stable and solid.*

Buddhist mountains because they often double as an image of one of two sacred creatures: turtles, which were thought to support Mount Horai on their backs, and cranes, on which the immortal sages were supposed to ride. Turtle rocks are quite common and are easily identified, though the turtle is usually represented only by one or other of its body parts — most often its outstretched neck and head, occasionally its legs, tail and shell. Sometimes the turtle is represented by a small island, with a rock in its center representing Mount Horai, and a pine, the tree sacred to Chinese sages, planted nearby. Cranes are usually represented by a stubby triangular stone signifying an outstretched wing. Occasionally stones are chosen to represent their long necks or their tails. Both turtle and crane rocks can be found in pond gardens and surrounded by sand in dry gardens.

Placing rocks

When making a garden, the first thing a Japanese considers is where the principal rock — the largest, most imposing, and beautiful one — should be placed. This is usually the most important decision, for everything else follows on from it. At Chion-in Temple, Kyoto, the smaller of the two gardens facing the hall holds twenty-six stones set among an undulating sea of clipped azaleas. One rock dominates the entire garden: this represents Buddha. When the azaleas are in bloom, it looks as though Buddha is descending in glory on shimmering clouds, accompanied by a host of bodhisattvas. The composition is borrowed from a painting preserved at Chion-in Temple. At Jizo-in Temple, also in Kyoto, sixteen stones represent monks who have attained serene enlightenment.

Rocks, or even large stones, are permanent features of Japanese gardens, so each one should be firmly set in the ground. In this way the garden soon takes on an ageless quality.

facing page: *The similarity of shape between the rocks and the pruned shrubs serves to highlight the differences between the inanimate and the living. This is an important though unobtrusive theme in many Zen rock gardens.*

Water

If rocks symbolize Japan's mountainous terrain, water in the garden represents the swift rivers and tranquil lakes of the country, and the broad seas by which she is surrounded. Islands in the middle of ponds and lakes, sometimes nothing more than a few outcrops of rock, reflect the country's self-image as an archipelago scattered across the open sea.

Ponds

Ponds tend to be irregular in shape, as the aim is to create a naturalistic look. However, there are certain shapes which caught the fanciful imagination of early gardening masters, and allowed them to add another layer of symbolism to their designs. One is the cloud shape, another is the bottle gourd. Then there are a couple of traditional shapes based on the calligraphic rendering of Chinese pictograms: one is the word for water, the other the word for spirit or soul. All of these flowing shapes produce an interestingly varied shoreline, and for this reason ponds and lakes have continued to be designed with them in mind.

The edges of a pond can be adorned with aquatic or marginal plants. The most popular by far are Japanese water irises: *Iris laevigata* and *I. ensata*. The latter needs to be kept out of water after it has finished flowering and over the winter. Plant irises in swathes for their handsome leaves and their purple, mauve, lavender or white blossoms. *Iris pseudacorus* (the yellow flag iris of Europe) and *Iris versicolor* (the blue flag iris of North America) are good alternatives. *Acorus calamus* (sweet flag or sweet rush), with its aromatic, slender leaves, is also very attractive; so is

its Japanese relation, *Acorus gramineus*. Further away from the shore, water-lilies can be grown in clumps so that their leaves eventually form green circles that contrast with the open water.

Do not allow aquatic plants to cover the entire pond. The pleasure of an open expanse of water is often enhanced by keeping the planting to a minimum and letting the water act as a mirror to the clouds, lanterns, rocks and waterside trees. In warmer climates *Nelumbo nucifera* (sacred lotus), perhaps the most perfect aquatic flower of all, can be grown in large garden ponds or lakes. The flowers of paradise in Buddhism, they have a unique elegance, holding their perfectly shaped, pointed buds high above their leaves; when the petals unfold, each one looks as though it has been cut from the most delicate silk. The flowers also have a marvellous scent.

right: *A* yatsuhashi *(zig-zag) bridge makes an ideal path through shallow water planted with aquatic and marginal plants. This low type of bridge helps to create the feeling that one is walking among the plants. It makes it possible to see up close the frilly delicacy and exquisite markings of* Iris ensata. *This example is from the Japanese Garden in Portland, Oregon.*

facing page: *Hill-and-pond stroll gardens can be designed to fit a surprising range of sizes. This is a very intimate example from the United States. Instead of a wooden ornamental bridge, a simple footbridge has been put together using stone slabs. Lanterns with curved legs are used exclusively over water.*

Perennials such as astilbe and filipendula, with their open sprays of flowers, and foliage plants, such as Astilboides tabularis *and* Rodgersia podophylla, *would suit the wet margins of informal ponds such as this one.*

facing page: *A boulder placed strategically at the bottom but slightly to one side of the sheet of water creates a spectacular cascade effect, which adds further interest and power to this waterfall.*

Creating sand-bars or a pebble or shingle beach is one of the oldest traditions in Japanese gardening. These can be made to resemble anything from a desolate seashore to the appealing bank of a pleasantly cool mountain lake. Sometimes a long headland of pebbles is created across a narrow section of a

shoreline. Craggier rocks and a jagged shore, on the other hand, create the feeling of wild, wave-swept sea cliffs. In these settings rocks should be used with discretion; too many will reduce the overall impact. It is important always to place them where they look as though they belong. When selecting rocks for water

above: *It is important to choose a lantern of a size and style that harmonizes with its surroundings. Here a yukimi lantern on legs stands among low-growing junipers, ferns, and rocks by the edge of a pond in a San Francisco garden. It is neither hidden among them nor too tall to draw attention away from them.*

pond, clearly referring to one of the most famous traditional sights along the Sea of Japan, a long sand spit known as Ama-no-hashidate or the Bridge to Heaven.

Large rocks are often arranged around the edge of ponds, particularly where a smooth bank of *Zoysia japonica* (Japanese carpet grass) descends right down to the water. These banks produce a mellow pastoral effect, especially if the pond is given a gently curving

features, try to find pieces which suggest the activity of water; for example, one convention involves placing a large, flattish boulder along the outer shore of a bend in a stream. The rock then looks as if it is actually directing the course of the water, and becomes an integral part of the design of the stream.

All these ways of embellishing a bank allow the gardener to create his or her own image of Nature while protecting the edge from erosion. Still, there are alternatives to a naturalistic approach. Low pine stakes, about 4 in (10 cm) in diameter, are often used along the edge of a pond or lake to give the shoreline definition. They do not need to be all the same height; instead they can be arranged so that their tops form a wavy line. Willow or split bamboo strips can be used to weave the poles together. A line of low poles of this kind is also used to distinguish areas where water irises are planted, so that they do not look too straggly.

Waterfalls

Waterfalls and cascades marry together the image of mountain heights with the attraction of flowing water. They can be thin or broad, overhanging or meandering, or broken by rocks. They may consist of two or three steps.

A basic arrangement of four rocks is traditionally used for waterfalls. The largest serves as the backdrop for the falling water, and it is supported by one boulder on each side . These can be flanked in turn by smaller rocks. At the base of the falls, a smoother rock protrudes slightly above the surface of the water; this indicates where the water hits the pool and helps to part the stream. Sometimes a rock for this spot was chosen to represent a carp, after a Chinese myth about a carp that climbed a waterfall and became a dragon that then rose up to Heaven. An extra couple of rocks can be placed further downstream to help indicate the direction of the flow. If a long, flat rock is being used as a bridge, it too should be placed slightly downstream so as not to block the view of the waterfall. Stepping-stones across the stream can be used instead. This arrangement can be used in dry gardens as well, for it is very effective with sand or fine gravel representing a flowing stream.

Ground-hugging vegetation is usually planted around the source of the water above the falls. To

conceal it further, an evergreen is placed at the top of the falling water. A Japanese maple, a pine or a weeping willow is usually planted next to the waterfall so that its branches partly conceal it. The sight of cascading water glimpsed through a veil of delicate foliage is often considered a finer thing than a completely exposed view, for it adds a sense of mystery and depth to the whole composition.

Creating water features

Designing a water feature is an integral part of deciding on an overall landscape for the garden. It might be a mountain pool surrounded by tall rocks and evergreen shrubs, or a lake in grassy open countryside. A waterfall, a spring-fed basin, a rippling brook or a lazy, winding stream — all are possibilities.

In a domestic garden, a water feature can be created by using convenient pre-formed ponds, which are readily available from garden suppliers. Some people may wish to design their own ponds, incorporating various planting schemes and groups of rocks. In these cases, the generally recommended way of securing the sides and the bottom of the pond is to use concrete over a bed of hardcore. When digging out the pond, it is important to allow for the combined thickness of the layers of hardcore and concrete. Check that the pond is level, using a plank and a spirit level. The layer of hardcore should be up to 6 in (15 cm) thick and firmly compacted. The concrete (1 part cement to 3 parts sand to 6 parts grit) goes on top of this and should be 4 in (10 cm) thick. Put in wire reinforcing mesh to strengthen the walls and bottom of the pond.

It is a good idea to have the walls of the pond sloping outwards, for this will ensure that the concrete will not crack if ice forms on the surface of the water. If the sides slope, it will probably also be possible to apply the concrete without using a frame. If the walls are perpendicular, however, a frame made

Setting a rock at the edge of a pool

right *If the pond is large, it is often easier to incorporate the ledge when first digging it out. Sloping, shallow edges will make it unnecessary to build a frame into which to pour the concrete. It is important to make sure that there are no cracks in the concrete or the mortar, particularly around the rocks.*

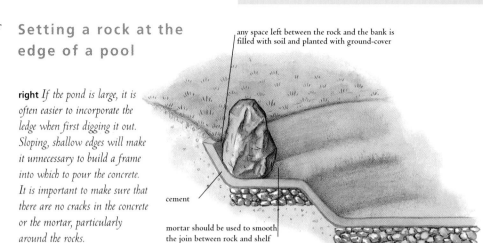

any space left between the rock and the bank is filled with soil and planted with ground-cover

cement

mortar should be used to smooth the join between rock and shelf

hardcore

Traditional pond shapes

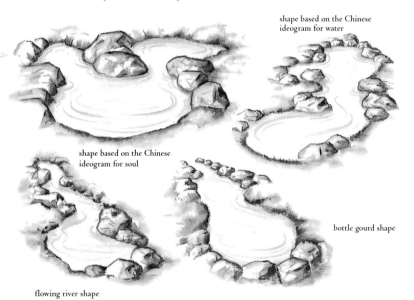

shape based on the Chinese ideogram for water

shape based on the Chinese ideogram for soul

bottle gourd shape

flowing river shape

cloud shape

facing page: *A pool fed by a cascade is an ideal spot for a sheltered bench. A wisteria pergola could be constructed instead, for it will have a cool canopy of light green leaves during the summer and earlier in the year it will be hung with clusters of blossom. Shades of purple look particularly striking when seen against a backdrop of green. They are very beautiful near water if used with restraint as they are here in the Honda Tea Garden designed by J. Dowle and K. Ninomiya for the Chelsea Flower Show in 1995 (the same garden is pictured on page 4). Various paths allow the garden to be seen from different perspectives.*

of plywood boards will be necessary as a mould into which to pour the concrete. Be sure to include an overflow in the design of the pond so that water will not spill out when there is heavy rain.

Underwater rocks can be secured to the bottom and sides of the pond on a bed of mortar (1 part cement to 4 parts sand). The layer of mortar should be up to 2 in (5 cm) thick. It is a good idea to paint some waterproofing agent onto the concrete before the mortar goes on (an alternative is to mix a water-proofing agent in with the concrete itself). Make sure when applying the mortar around the rocks that there are no cracks left through which the water can seep away. If there are any gaps above the water level between the rocks and the concrete, fill them in with earth. When the construction is finished, apply a sealant to the surface of the mortar to keep harmful lime from leaching into the water. Setting up groups of rocks at the edge of the water might be easier in a deep pond if there is a shelf along its rim so that the rocks can be placed in shallower water. A shelf of this kind also comes in handy for positioning aquatic plants. The pond can be dug out with various levels already incorporated, or the shelf can be built after-wards using breeze blocks. Rocks in the middle of the pond can be fixed to the bottom with mortar. A larger island for planting azaleas or even a pine can be left in place when the pond is first being dug. Remember that its sides must be waterproofed in the same way as the rest of the pond.

If the pond is intended for fish, round off any sharp edges underwater using mortar so that the fish will not injure themselves against either the sides of the pond or the rocks. Avoid releasing fish into a freshly made pond as the chemical agents in the concrete might kill them off. Leave the water to rest for a few days after construction before putting in any plants as well. Fish should not be introduced until two or more weeks after the plants.

above: *Here the designer Richard Coward juxtaposes the straight lines of the decking in the foreground with the curved shoreline created at the other end of the garden by the plants, such as the clump of* Iris laevigata.

For an average garden, the pool should not be more than 20 to 24 in (50 to 60 cm) deep, although if it is intended for big koi carp it will have to be deeper than the length of the full-grown fish. On the other hand, it can be as shallow as 12 in (30 cm). Where the bottom of the pool is visible, embed pebbles in the mortar for a more natural look. A simple way of adding aquatic and marginal plants to a pond is to use purpose-made containers, which are made of lattice-work to allow water to circulate. Containers with a coarse mesh should be lined with hessian or close-woven polypropylene sheets so that soil is not washed out. These containers can rest on the bottom of the pool or, if the plants are marginals, on a shelf around the edge of the pond. As some aquatic plants require ever-deeper water as they begin to grow from spring onwards, it is easier to adjust their depth if they sit on blocks, which can be removed as necessary. Use specialist aquatic compost or garden soil enriched with bonemeal and top-dress with gravel.

Creating a stream

When designing a stream, try to visualize the direction in which the current is flowing. A shallow, pebbly brook, for example, might develop eventually into a broad, gentle stream. A more mountainous one might have its beginnings in a waterfall or a series of small cascades. Rocks placed in the middle of a current need to look as though they belong there, and pebbly shoals should seem as though they were naturally created by the flowing water. Rocks which are carefully positioned in this way can help to emphasize the feeling of moving water.

A stream should be between 12 and 16 in (30 to 40 cm) deep with waterside plants and rocks to evoke the idea of a natural running stream. Alter-natively, it could be very shallow, with water barely 2 in (5 cm) deep. If the bottom is then covered with

Laying a stream bed

hardcore

concrete

shrub

stone parting the current

mortar

gravel about 1 in (2 cm) in diameter, the water will produce a pleasant, soothing murmur.

Streams are constructed in the same way as ponds. If it is to be a shallow stream with slow-flowing water, the concrete can be poured after the rocks have already been set in place. Use gravel or pebbles for the bottom of the stream, embedding about a third of the material into the mortar. The remainder can be used to conceal any mortar still visible. This will ensure that the entire stream bed will not shift around in the flowing water.

It is important that there should be something in the garden suggesting the head, or source, of the stream. It could be a waterfall; shrubs can be used to disguise the header pool at the top where the water is piped in. Or the water can be made to run out from between rocks to suggest a mountain spring. Another method is to have water trickling from a bamboo spout into a stone basin which then overflows into a little rill. This arrangement is likewise meant to suggest a naturally flowing spring, and it should be designed and planted with this in mind. The actual amount of water from the bamboo spout will not be sufficient to create a current, so supplement your stream with water from another concealed source.

By giving your stream curves and bends, it will be possible to experiment with perspective in order to

give depth to your garden. By having the water level between 4 and 8 in (10 to 20 cm) lower than ground level, the brook itself will look deeper. The eye will be drawn to strategically placed rocks along its bank, or to dotted specimen trees – Japanese maples, for instance, or birches in a larger garden. The feeling of open space can be produced by planting ground-hugging plants like *Ophiopogon* or moss, or by putting stepping-stones across the stream. A solitary weeping Japanese maple can veil a bend in a winding stream in a way that adds mystery to the garden. Its impact is diminished, however, if it has to fight for attention with other plants. A tree leaning over a pool or shrubs that barely trail their leaves over the water helps to soften the lines of the stream or pond. It is not nearly as effective to overcrowd the banks with many different plants.

It is important to keep in mind where the vantage points in your garden are going to be, for you are designing the garden to be viewed and appreciated from these spots. Make sure that your stream is not entirely obscured either by the terrain (from the

above: *Where the bed of a stream is visible, it is important to make it decorative by putting in a layer of pebbles. A third should be embedded in the mortar so they cannot shift around in the flowing water. The rest should completely cover any exposed areas of mortar. A cascade can be incorporated into a stream by adapting the basic design used for constructing waterfalls. The rock over which the water flows is flanked on either side by slightly taller stones, each of which has in turn a shorter, chunkier stone at its base. A leaf-shaped stone is placed slightly downstream of a waterfall or cascade to divide the current. It should rise out of the water in the direction of the falling water and taper at the other end.*

A shrub, such as Callicarpa dichotoma *– or a maple, willow, or pine in the case of a waterfall – should be planted by the falling water so that its branches partly veil it, softening the contours of the rocks.*

stream lying too low below ground level) or by the planting. If it is a small garden, the primary vantage point is inevitably going to be from the house. A stream that flows near the house will be much more interesting than one that remains in the far distance. A stream 1 to 2 ft (30 to 60 cm) wide is said to look its best from a distance of about 10 to 20 ft (3 to 6 m) away. In a larger garden, the stream can be as much as 3 ft 3 in to 5 ft (1 to 1.5 m) in width. If a path leads to views of the garden, plan it so that the scenery changes steadily. Surprise your visitors. A partly concealed feature will excite their curiosity, and a turn in the path can suddenly open up an unexpected view.

To have water circulating in the garden, it will be necessary to create a pool at the bottom of the watercourse in which a submersible pump can be installed. Water can then be pumped back up to the top of the watercourse through a flexible pipe buried under the soil (and protected by a row of narrow tiles placed on top of it so that it cannot be accidentally punctured by a probing spade). If the top end of the pipe is to be submerged in the header pool, the pipe will need to be fitted with a non-return valve so that water cannot flow the wrong way. A header pool at the top of the watercourse will also help to reserve water and minimize its loss when the pump is turned off. A series of cascades with each step slightly inclining towards the back will create little pools which will also retain water.

If you are going to have miniature cascades, the gradient of the stream bed should be between eight and ten per cent; if the stream is to be a slow flowing one, the gradient can be between one and two per cent. The longer the stream is, the higher the source of water will need to be elevated in order to create a current. Since a stone basin is usually placed on low ground, it could look out of place if perched on top of a mound to disguise the source of a watercourse,

unless a method is devised to deceive the eye so that the ground does not seem as high as it actually is. Use a low basin and make the ground slope as gently as possible. Otherwise, plants can be used to minimize the impression of height.

When planning any kind of water feature, it is absolutely necessary to keep in mind the safety of

children who might be visiting your garden. It is important to remember that traditional Japanese-style gardens are not designed to be safe play-areas for children.

Decking is a good way of creating a low verandah that overlooks a water garden. Pruned shrubs may be used in front of low verandahs so that the drop to the level of the garden will not seem so abrupt.

facing page: A series of shallow cascades produces a delightfully cool feeling in hot climates. Japan is exceedingly hot and humid in summer and people yearn for the sight and sound of cool mountain streams.

above: Water rushing among a cluster of rocks broadens into a gentle, smooth-flowing stream with a broad, pebbly shoreline which makes it look wider than it really is.

facing page: *Branches of mature trees and bushes soften the line of a pond, giving it a sense of depth.*

above: *Water rushes from a bamboo spout into a stone basin and overflows into a pond. The basin is natural rock and looks as though it has been carved by the flow of water. This design expresses vividly the idea of a mountain spring.*

Stone basins

For intimate gardens too small for a pond, a water feature that incorporates a basin may be an attractive alternative. Stone basins are a particularly important feature of tea gardens and were originally meant for washing the hands and rinsing the mouth. Even if they are primarily meant to be decorative, they should still look practical and be provided with a *hishaku*, a bamboo scoop used for pouring water over the hands. They can be hollowed-out natural stone or elaborately sculpted in any number of traditional styles. Popular shapes include the Japanese apricot (*ume*), easily identifiable by its five rounded petals, and the multi-petalled chrysanthemum. Another familiar type is the *natsume*, a tall but squat cylindrical basin, named after the fruit of the jujube tree (*Ziziphus jujuba*) which it is said to resemble. Circular coin shapes are also common, some with Chinese characters in bas relief around the mouth: one type is called *fusen* after the Chinese coin on which it is modelled. Another, named after the Ryoan-ji Temple where its famous prototype is found, has four Chinese characters around a square mouth, the message reading "The only important thing is to know to be content." Square basins include the *ginkakuji* style, which has lattice patterns on three of its sides. Other square basins have Buddhas carved in bas relief instead, referring back to a time when old pieces of temple masonry were rescued and reused as water basins in tea gardens.

Setting up stone basins once again involves traditional arrangements of rocks called *tsukubai*. The basin is set low and placed next to a sump to catch overflowing water. This sump is sometimes called the "ocean". It may have pebbles embedded in its mortar lining and a few free stones concealing the drainage hole. Sometimes four or five rough stones are piled up above the hole instead, but they need to be placed so that water does not splash the user. The larger the

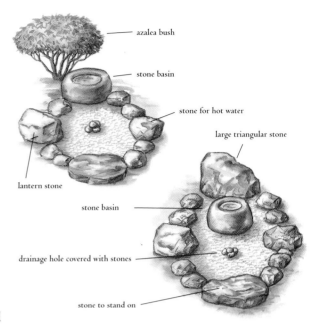

azalea bush

stone basin

stone for hot water

large triangular stone

lantern stone

stone basin

drainage hole covered with stones

stone to stand on

Stone basin arrangements

basin the shallower and wider the sump needs to be. A small basin can be placed on a short stand inside a deeper sump; however, the sump must not be deeper than any sewage system it might be connected to, so that drainage is not impeded.

Opposite the basin and across the sump, a flat, low stone provides a place stable and broad enough for an adult to stand on comfortably. This stone is generally placed at a distance of about 2 ft 4 in (70 cm) from the middle of the basin, and is larger and slightly higher than the other stepping-stones in the garden. To the right of this stone, traditional *tsukubai* will have a slightly taller flat stone where, in cold weather, a basin of hot water was placed for the use of guests attending the tea ceremony. On the left is a flat stone, again taller than the stone for the hot-water basin, where a lantern would be left for evening ceremonies. The positions of these last two stones are reversed in other traditions of the tea ceremony. A large, tall stone or an evergreen shrub is sometimes placed behind the basin to give height to the overall arrangement and to provide a sense of protection.

Sand

right: *Here at the Bloedel Reserve, Bainbridge Island, Washington, a flat, abstract, dry garden is successfully integrated with an open landscaped garden. There is no feeling that a fence is necessary to create a special "Japanese" area. The abstract arrangement of the rocks contains three distinct groups. The one in the foreground illustrates the basic scalene triangle layout of three rocks.*

Along with running water, the simplicity of white sand evokes a sense of calm and purity in the garden. White sand has always been used in the gardens of both Shinto shrines and Buddhist temples to mark off a sacred ritual space. Sand is thus a way of bringing a spiritual dimension into the garden without reference to any specific religion. It has a significant part to play in many types of Japanese gardens. Where there may not be enough space for a water feature, sand can represent a river, a lake or even an ocean, with the added boon of eliminating the need to worry about waterproofing. More importantly, white sand can create a sense of open space in the smallest and darkest courtyard garden.

In the ancient gardens of Kyoto, the sand used was not sea sand but fine, white, decomposed granite gravel. For a sand garden, choose coarse sand or gravel with grains between ⅛ to ⅜ in (3 and 8 mm) in diameter. Obviously, sand that is too fine will blow around in the wind. Another reason for avoiding sea sand is that its smooth, round grains will not stay in place when it is raked into a pattern. An important thing to check when buying sand or gravel is its color, both when it is dry and when it is wet.

The first step in creating a sand feature is to make the ground smooth and level. Firm the soil by rolling it well and then put in a layer of coarse gravel. On top of this goes a layer of concrete or mortar to a depth of about 2 in (5 cm). This will help to keep the sand clean and unmuddied and prevents the growth of weeds. It is important that the concrete should be provided with drainage points for

rainwater to escape, either by seeping into the gravel layer or by draining away through a pipe. Another possibility, if the area is a small one, is to use a polypropylene sheet with holes punched into it at regular intervals. If the sand gets dirty, it can easily be hosed down. For edging the sand garden a variety of materials are used, including brick, stone, paving tiles and wood, but try to avoid plastic. The sand is laid to a depth of between 1 ¼ and 4 in (3 and 10 cm), depending on whether or not patterns are to be raked in it. The underlying concrete or polypropylene sheet must not be exposed by the patterns, which should be at least 2 in (5 cm) in depth to look effective, though they can be deeper.

Before the pattern is raked in, the sand is swept, preferably with a besom, and levelled with an implement consisting of a board attached to a long handle. Common garden rakes are now generally used for making the patterns, but many famous temples

concentric ripples

whirlpool

ocean wave

Traditional sand patterns

sideways concentric ripples

open river wave

surf pattern

stream current

have their own specially designed wooden or bamboo rakes. There are quite a number of traditional sand patterns to choose from, and there is nothing to stop the gardener from experimenting with an original design. Traditional motifs are often based on the theme of waves. Sand is used like this in dry Zen gardens to symbolize the perpetual motion of water. Parallel, gently undulating lines can suggest a calm brook, river or ocean, depending on the width of the lines. Some designs are naturalistic, others highly stylized. There is one popular pattern representing high ocean waves which is often mistaken in the West for fish scales; it is also found as a design on fabric or paper. Whorls and spirals signify whirlpools. By raking concentric circles around a rock, it can be made to look like either a miniature outcrop of land in the middle of a minute ocean or, at the same time, a pebble or even a leaf which has just fallen into a pool of water.

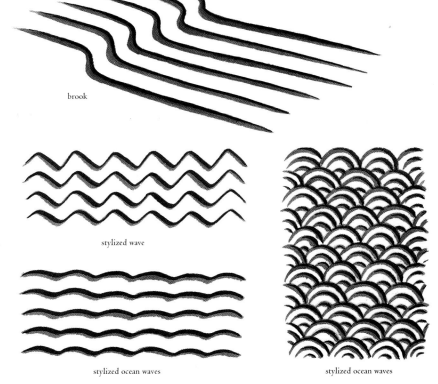

brook

stylized wave

stylized ocean waves

stylized ocean waves

Paths and stepping-stones

Stepping-stones were first used in tea gardens to provide paths while preserving the naturalistic ambience of the planting. When set in moss or among low, ground-hugging plants, stepping-stones succeed in blurring the boundaries between the planting and the path. Rather than banishing humans to footpaths, it draws people into the garden. Even when stepping-stones are meant primarily to be decorative, like stone basins they should always appear functional. Japanese gardens have evolved various stylized forms over the centuries, but each feature originally had a practical purpose which even now should not be forgotten. There is beauty in a tool which fulfils its purpose. Stepping-stones set too close next to a hedge or those which lead nowhere at all are unseemly, even if they are only meant to be ornamental. So are stones which are too far apart, awkwardly placed, or too rounded at the top.

Stepping-stones should be flat and at least 8 to 12 in (20 to 30 cm) in diameter to make walking easy and safe. Try to avoid stones which are indented towards the center as they will collect water. They should be at least 4 in (10 cm) in thickness, and should rise between 1 ¼ to 3 ½ in (3 and 9 cm) above ground level (lower for tea gardens, higher for domestic gardens). The art of laying out stepping-stones made of natural rock lies in the skill of juxtaposing their irregular shapes against each other in such a way that they also look pleasing.

The stones are generally placed 4 in (10 cm) apart, but this depends on the size of the stones.

Calculate how far apart to set your stones, based on the length of your stride. In Japan, 1 ft 8 in (50 cm) is the usual distance allowed between the center of one stepping-stone and the next. In tea gardens, however, a pace is considered to be slightly shorter. Anything farther apart makes walking in Japanese dress difficult. Contrary to popular notions in the West, kimonos are not loose-flowing garments. They are very tightly secured around the midriff, not with a flimsy sash, but a thick and solid length of silk. Women are expected to walk decorously without letting the skirts of their kimonos fly open. The use of traditional slippers – the thongs of which pass between the big toe and the adjoining toe – means that women tend to walk pigeon-toed as well, although men are allowed to stride a little more. All of this has implications for the way traditional

zig-zag patterns for stepping-stones have evolved.

If you have stones of different sizes, one idea is to alternate the large stones with smaller ones, keeping the distance between the centers of adjacent stones the same all the way along. Sometimes small ornamental stones are included in the design of the path. Oval stones are not only set lengthwise in the direction of the path, as might be expected, but often

also horizontally to avoid overemphasizing the forward movement of the path. Another thing to avoid is having right angles where paths intersect. A stone slightly bigger than the rest can be placed on the spot where paths diverge; this will also provide an attractive vantage-point in the garden. A prized specimen tree or a stone lantern is often placed near such a spot. Larger, more imposing stones are also

above: *Rocks and foliage plants are used almost exclusively here to experiment with different heights and textures. The clump of spiky irises in the foreground will provide a spot of bright color in the garden in spring.*

left: *Stones of different sizes and shapes have been meticulously fitted together to form this imposing path leading from the front gate to the entrance of Ryugen-in Temple, belonging to the Daitoku-ji Temple complex in Kyoto.*

Symmetry has been carefully avoided in the design of this garden. A solitary boulder to the left deceives the visitor into feeling that the garden is deeper than it really is. The doorway is partly hidden behind the trees.

Though the planting is almost entirely restricted to evergreens, Osmanthus fragrans f. aurantiacus *in this kind of situation will give a heady scent in the autumn.*

Patterns for stepping-stones

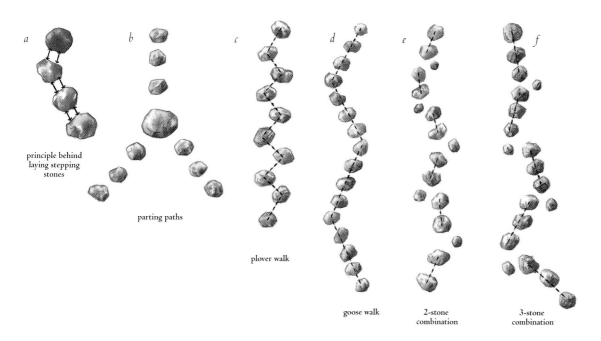

a

principle behind
laying stepping
stones

b

parting paths

c

plover walk

d

goose walk

e

2-stone
combination

f

3-stone
combination

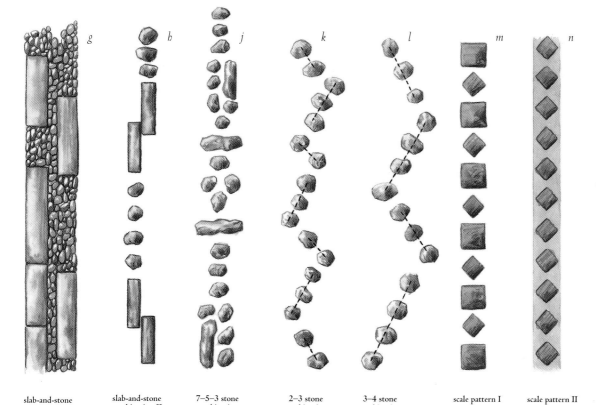

g

slab-and-stone
combination I

h

slab-and-stone
combination II

j

7–5–3 stone
combination

k

2–3 stone
combination

l

3–4 stone
combination

m

scale pattern I

n

scale pattern II

left: *Stepping-stones should be placed so that straight edges face each other and are roughly parallel (a). This is done so that the path looks the same width along its whole length. If two angular edges of adjacent stones face each other, the path will look as though it narrows at that point. Unless a stone is perfectly circular, it will have edges which are more or less straight.*

Where a path divides, a large flat stone, occasionally of a different type such as a millstone, is used as a decorative feature (b). This stone should be large enough for a person to stand on comfortably.

The plover (c) and goose (d) patterns are the basic zig-zag patterns used for stepping-stone paths. The 2–3 stone and 3–4 stone combination patterns (k and l) are adaptations of these. The 2-stone and 3-stone combinations (e and f) are designed to make the patterns as inconspicuous as possible. These are particularly good for tea gardens, where the path meanders among trees and shrubs.

The slab-and-stone combination I (g) can be used for formal paths leading up to a gate or an entrance, while the 7–5–3 combination (j) and slab-and-stone combination II (h) are suitable for a stretch of open ground. Scale patterns I (m) and II (n) can be used across open ground. Scale pattern I (m) can also make a graceful curved path. Kobori Enshu made it famous, using it across sand in the garden at Konchi-in, Nanzen-ji Temple, Kyoto.

laid near the house where there might be some open ground; a stone of some height is usually provided as a step down from the verandah.

After the stepping-stones have been set in the ground, they can be surrounded by gravel or sand, or moss may be allowed to grow between them. For a more formal straight path, however, a combination of smaller stones with rectangular paving stones set in a geometrical pattern makes a very handsome alternative. This kind of paving is suitable for paths that will be in continual heavy use, and is therefore often employed for walks within temple and shrine compounds. It is ideal for paths leading up to the front door. It is rather like cobblestones, but the individual stones are flatter and therefore less painful for the ankles and the soles of the feet.

Where the stones are thick, they are set directly in mortar (I part cement to 2.5 to 3 parts sand) which has been spread on a bed of gravel. If they are thin, the bed of gravel is first set with concrete 4 in (10 cm) deep, on top of which the mortar is laid after the concrete has been allowed to dry for a day or two. When the stones are of both kinds, the thicker ones are set first, using the former technique, after which the remaining spaces are filled with the thinner kind, using the concrete method. This type of path looks striking when edged with gravel.

left: *Although pines and ever-greens form the backbone of most traditional Japanese gardens, maples are often used near paths for the pleasant dappled shade they give throughout the spring, summer, and autumn months. On a crisp autumn day drifts of crimson maple leaves, each starry shape distinct against a deep blue sky, look as though they are floating on water.*

facing page: *A traditional* roji, *or tea garden, helps to re-create the feeling of a rustic Japanese retreat in a mountain forest. The planting is very informal. The path picks its way through lush ferns and* Farfugium japonicum, *which help to reinforce the sense of seclusion and privacy. This garden belongs to the Tabuchi family of Ako, Japan.*

Bridges

right: *Natural stone used as stepping-stones across a shallow stream looks inviting, especially during the hot summer months. Choosing flat stones and making certain that they are laid out at equal intervals ensures that they are safe to use without looking contrived.*

Stepping-stones can be used across shallow running water for a naturalistic effect, but several kinds of bridges have traditionally been used for various kinds of formal gardens.

The humpback wooden bridge with vermilion-colored railings is very well-known. It needs to be employed with caution lest the bright color over-whelms everything else in the garden. It works best in large gardens, where it can be seen from a distance, its bold color and shape softened by the planting of a delicate weeping willow or a Japanese maple by the foot of the bridge. In Japan these bridges were a part of the aristocratic gardens of the tenth and eleventh centuries, which were created around lakes and little islands. Keep the vermilion bridge for a special scenic spot in the garden.

Elegant wooden bridges, either humpbacked or straight, were also used to connect islands in those aristocratic lake gardens of Kyoto, and in the hill and lake stroll gardens of later periods. They were often designed to produce a pleasing reflection in the deep water of the lake. Where the pond was planted with water irises, rushes and water-lilies, a zig-zag (*yatsuhashi*) bridge was a favorite. This type of bridge is still very popular; it is best described as a narrow boardwalk with wooden planks set out in a zig-zag pattern across the pond or lake. Being a low bridge, it allows people to stroll literally among the plants growing in the water.

Types of humpback bridge other than the vermilion variety can be less obtrusive and over-whelming in a smaller garden. Made of either logs or wooden planks, and varnished to bring out the natural hue of the wood, they can enhance the rustic feel of Japanese gardens. They can even be made of turf, supported on a tier of logs, then one of bamboo and finally a sheet of zinc. A turf bridge should not have railings. Generally speaking, short bridges look better if they do not have prominent high railings, though, of course, when planning a bridge, the safety of those using the garden must come first.

Whereas turf and other humpback bridges are particularly good in gardens with dense, low ground-cover, simpler bridges are used in moss gardens and rock gardens. These usually consist of nothing more than a long, flat slab of rock, sometimes anchored at each end with a pair of stones of different heights. Bridges of rock are ideal for narrow streams in small-

scale gardens, where a wooden bridge with railings
might look out of proportion. They are also used in
dry gardens over streams represented by sand or a
bed of pebbles. Two slabs of rock can be arranged
end to end and supported in the middle by a tall
boulder to form a single span over a slightly wider,
shallow stream.

Single pieces of cut stone, often with a slight
curve, are sometimes used in tea gardens instead of

natural stone. These are now becoming available in
the West as well, and they can be a very good alternative to naturally weathered rock, though their hard,
straight lines give them a slightly artificial feeling.
These types of stone bridge are traditionally used
near waterfalls and cascades, whether dry or in full
flow. They suited the Zen taste for rugged, austere
representations of nature in the garden, and were
adopted in the intimate stroll gardens of Zen temples.

above: *A* yatsuhashi *bridge is
extremely informal. The
handrail does not extend along
the whole length of the bridge,
but only where the designer
thinks someone might want to
pause and take in the view.*

left: *This area of "An Oriental Garden", designed by NJ Landscapes for the Malvern Show, 1998, gives a good idea of the design of a yatsuhashi bridge, though this example is more ornamental than practical. The zig-zag design comes into its own when it is used to cross wide sections of shallow water or boggy or swampy land.*

above: *An ornamental humpback bridge is usually made of wood but is sometimes available in stone or even concrete. For a short bridge in a small garden the simplest design is the best. Here the ornamental touches have been restricted to the posts. Pink sea thrift has been used to evoke the feeling of a rocky terrain.*

Types of bridges

right: *A turf bridge is supported by a row of logs secured to two crosspieces which run the whole length of the bridge. A tier of bamboo canes is constructed on top of the row of logs. A sheet of thin metal supports the soil, which should be slightly banked up along the edges of the bridge. Lay turf so that its root system will hold the soil in place.*

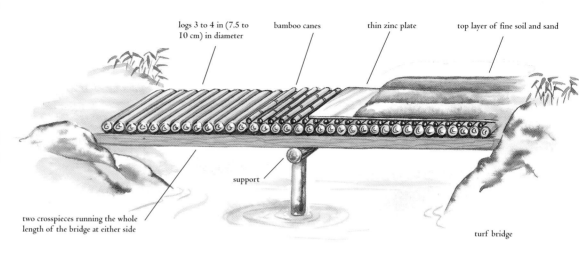

logs 3 to 4 in (7.5 to 10 cm) in diameter

bamboo canes

thin zinc plate

top layer of fine soil and sand

support

two crosspieces running the whole length of the bridge at either side

turf bridge

above: *A clever inversion has been used here: the moss represents the stream and the gravel dry land. Pine logs have been woven together with twine to construct a raft-like bridge. A structure of this kind forms the foundation of turf bridges. Chinese balloon flower (Platy-codon grandiflorum) in very small, isolated clumps can be planted among moss to replicate how Iris laevigata would grow by a real stream.*

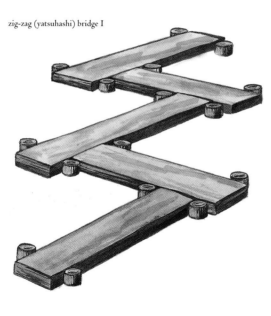

zig-zag (yatsuhashi) bridge I

left: *Zig-zag bridges are usually constructed of wooden planks, which are supported by horizontal struts held in place between two piles. It is important to make sure that bridges, if they are to be more than ornamental, are sturdy enough to bear the weight of humans. Professional advice from firms specializing in the construction of bridges is recommended.*

below: *The zig-zag pattern can be modified to suit a particular garden. This style is better than style I for crossings over shallow streams. It can also be built with cut stone. Cut-stone bridges are often used in tea gardens; single-span bridges of this type often have a slight curve to them. Being stone bridges, they are usually flanked by a pair of rocks of differing heights at either end.*

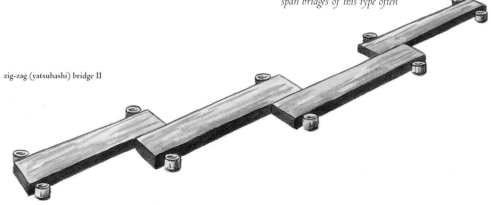

zig-zag (yatsuhashi) bridge II

left: *A short yatsuhashi-type bridge can be made with stone slabs instead of wooden planks. Quarried stone is better suited to this geometric bridge than, for instance, a natural-looking foot-bridge of the type illustrated on page 37. This example is from a New England garden, designed and owned by Fred Watson.*

Stone lanterns

Votive stone lanterns have always embellished roads and paths leading to Shinto shrines and Buddhist temples. They combined utility with beauty and were often donated by the faithful. On certain ceremonial days, many of these lanterns are still lighted with tiny candles, the windows screened with rice-paper; they illuminate the way for worshippers attending an evening rite.

Lanterns were brought into the garden in the sixteenth century with the development of the tea garden. Although the greatest tea master, Sen-no-Rikyu, is said to have introduced them into his tea gardens because he admired the distant flicker of their light, lanterns served the dual purposes of ornamenting the garden and guiding guests on their way to an evening tea ceremony. Nowadays they are more often decorative, but they should be positioned with their original purpose in mind. They can, for instance, be placed near a *tsukubai*, if the basin does not possess a stone for a hand-held lantern.

There are four main types of stone lantern and their uses differ slightly. The standard lantern has both a shaft and a pedestal. This is known as the *tachi-gata*, or standing lantern. Many of these are named after ancient temples, where their prototypes are still found. The best-known is the six-sided lantern found at, and named after, the Kasuga Shrine in Nara. These lanterns tend to be large and elaborately carved, making them rather ponderous. Still, they have dignity and poise, and they can be imposing when placed near paths, gates or entrances, or against tall shrubbery. They can be complemented with a pine-tree, *Ilex integra*, *I. crenata* (box-leaved holly), *Ternstroemia gymnanthera*, *Taxus cuspidata* (Japanese yew), *Torreya nucifera* (Japanese nutmeg yew) or *Viburnum japonicum*. The elegance of Japanese maples, *Ilex serrata* (Japanese winterberry) and *Euonymus alatus* (winged euonymus) creates a pleasing contrast to the gravity of this type of lantern.

A more modest type of lantern lacks the pedestal. Called *ikegomi-gata*, these lanterns are stuck straight into the ground. They look effective against less dense planting in the inner or courtyard garden. They also show up well against gravel and sand; their simpler form suits a more austere atmosphere. The appealing simplicity of their shape makes them appropriate for tea gardens as well, and for use next to low stone basins. The most famous design of this kind is the *oribe-gata*, easily recognized by the round bulge on its shaft.

The third type, the *oki-gata*, lacks the shaft. These are placed on flat stones. In wet and dry gardens

alike, a lantern of this type standing, or rather sitting, on a piece of land jutting out into the water produces a pleasing illusion of a lighthouse perched on a promontory.

The last type of lantern has legs. It can be octagonal, hexagonal or circular in shape and can have two, three, four or more legs. The best-known is the *yukimi-gata*, particularly attractive when seen in snow. Shorter and more compact than lanterns with shafts, they are also excellent for use next to water.

Other kinds of lanterns have one or more long, curved shafts. These are used specifically to lean over water. There are also rectangular stone lanterns in the shape of old-fashioned Japanese road signs

(*michi-shirube*); the light is placed behind a lattice window at the top. These should be placed at intervals along a path. Another variety is the pagoda, which can have between three and eleven tiers, so long as it is an odd number. Pagodas are available in different styles, some with hardly any space between the tiered roofs; these are more in the native style than those with ornamented windows, which are pseudo-Chinese. The best place to put a tall pagoda is up a slope in a far corner of the garden, where it will be very effective in creating the illusion of distance. In a flat garden, a bulky pagoda needs tall, slender trees and dense shrubs around it so that it does not look too bare and exposed.

above: *A round oki-gata lantern is typically placed at the end of a pebbly spit of land jutting out into water. One of the most important examples in Japan can be seen at the Katsura Imperial Palace outside Kyoto. The effect can be re-created in very restricted spaces as it works equally well in dry gardens. This example is in a garden in Augsburg, Germany.*

Pergolas

right: *Wisteria pergolas can be built over garden streams, ponds or a path as in this garden, Plantbessin, located in the Basse-Normandie region of France. Its creators, Colette and Hubert Sainte-Beuve, have constructed a wisteria pergola at the intersection of two paths. The pergola blends well with a Western-style planting scheme.*

The graceful, lavender-purple racemes of wisteria have an almost Edwardian elegance when draped over pale stone or red brick. These days, the idea of growing wisteria as a standard has also become widely accepted in the West. Indeed, surprisingly enough, wisteria can flower happily in a large pot as long as it is carefully pruned so that it does not outgrow the restricted amount of nutrient available.

In Japan, wisteria is generally trained carefully along a pergola. This is ideal for *Wisteria floribunda* (Japanese wisteria) as its racemes can be up to 2 ft (60 cm) long. *Wisteria chinensis* produces slightly shorter racemes of between 8 and 12 in (20 to 30 cm). In early summer, the pergola becomes a canopy of cascading blooms. There are very old and famous wisterias trained in this fashion all over Japan, and pergolas of this type hold a place of distinction in the garden. They should never have to compete for attention. They are given pride of place, uncrowded by other plants, perhaps set against a sedate, deep green backdrop of shapely pines. The trunk is also considered a beautiful asset of the plant — the more so the older the plant. Wisteria is planted against a pergola in such a way that the shape of the entire plant can be seen and admired when in flower and even when it is not. The wisteria is often surrounded by clean, white gravel, accompanied by a simple seat under the pergola. This seat, with no back or armrests, will be a simple slab of stone or a cross-section of a tree-trunk, highly polished so its age rings gleam.

For the posts and cross-beams of the pergola, *hinoki* cypress logs are generally used. They are treated with creosote or a similar preservative to stop them rotting — traditionally, the surface of the wood was charred, then brought to a high polish. Using poles for this frame rather than sawn timber creates a more rustic look, and is preferable for smaller pergolas holding one or two plants. The posts are connected to each other at the top with cross-beams. The pergola should be at least 8 ft 4 in (2.5 m) high.

The bamboo trellis secured to the top of this wooden frame is characteristic of Japanese-style pergolas. The trellis is composed of vertical and horizontal canes of bamboo, 2 in (5 cm) or slightly less in diameter and secured with wire, which are placed at 1 ft (30 cm) — occasionally up to 1 ft 6 in (45 cm) — intervals to form a lattice pattern. Using bamboo that is too thick will make the pergola seem top-heavy. Usually a space covering six or seven canes

— about 6 ft 8 in (2 m) — is allowed between two supporting wooden posts. The trellis should extend beyond the end of the wooden cross-pieces by the length of one interval between canes.

The overall impression should be one of lightness, but the pergola must be sturdy enough to bear the considerable weight of fully-grown wisterias.

Wisteria tends to take a long time to bloom,

although "Issai" varieties flower sooner than more traditional ones. From spring onwards, wisteria produces long shoots, which should be cut back late in summer. Leave some of them in the first two years to cover the trellis. In January or February these shoots are pruned back to between 1 ft and 3 ft 3 in (30 cm to 1 m). The plant then produces short spurs with flower-buds.

above: *From another direction, wisteria in full bloom forms a dramatic entrance to the oriental section of the garden. Wisteria pergolas can serve as delightful, informal arbors. A pergola is also an effective way of presenting some specimen plants in a large garden.*

Fences

right: *The slender grace of bamboo is brought out by the Japanese custom of carefully removing the lower branches from cultivated bamboo. This produces the special cool serenity of a bamboo grove or forest. The bushy leaves high overhead form a canopy that shuts out the remorseless summer sun, and everything below is still and calm in an eerie green light.*

facing page: *Branches of* kuro-moji *(Japanese spice-bush) form a choice material for rustic-style fences (see also page 118). The lacquered reddish-black tone of their bark lends particular elegance to a country garden. The branches have been patiently arranged back to front and in overlapping rows secured with horizontal bamboo struts.*

Fences become a prominent feature of a garden the smaller it is. In keeping with other features of the Japanese-style garden, natural materials are always preferable to artificial ones. The most important of these is, unsurprisingly, bamboo. Many varieties of bamboo are harvested for various purposes in Japan, therefore it can be obtained in different thicknesses. Thicker grades of bamboo up to 6 in (15 cm) across are becoming available in the West as well. Bamboo fences are meant to be impermanent; they are allowed to weather and are replaced every five years or so.

Another characteristic of Japanese garden fences is that the use of nails is avoided as much as possible. The fences are usually woven, or bound together using a rope traditionally made of hemp-palm fiber. This rope is black, and gives distinctive touches of color to these fences.

Bamboo fences can either be open-weave or close-weave; the choice of style depends on how much privacy is desired. Open-weave fences tend to be short, and they are used to mark off planted areas in the garden. The basic fence of this type is the *yotsume*, or four-eyed fence, composed of interwoven horizontal and vertical poles. The *kinkakuji* fence, named after the famous Golden Pavilion Temple in Kyoto, has a similar square weave, but it is distinguished by being crowned with split bamboo. The *yarai* and *ryoanji* styles are both diagonal weaves, the latter again having a split bamboo top.

The close-weave fence obviously gives more privacy than the open-weave types. It is as good as a screen, and is used, often in combination with rows

of tall conifers or evergreens, to mark the outer boundaries of a large garden. It may not be possible then to appreciate the fence from the house, but this kind of fence, being very elegant and decorative, may be one of the least ugly or offensive ways of putting up a high barrier between private property and a public road. Sometimes a close-weave fence is placed in front of tall trees or shrubs in such a way that their upper branches can still be seen above it. Over-hanging branches can help to soften the austere straight lines of this type of fence. They are particularly attractive if the trees are flowering ones. If a bough leans into a garden, the fence is simply built round it.

The *kenninji* fence is one of the most frequently seen. It is a high fence of split bamboo woven closely together in a single row along horizontal struts, which are thick bamboo canes split in half. These struts, which can be either four or five in number

(four is common in the west of Japan and five in the east) form the back of the fence. Halved lengths of bamboo are also set horizontally along the front of the fence to hide the rope-work that holds it together. These struts, unlike those at the back, are meant to be ornamental and are secured to the fence with neat knots at wide but regular intervals. For a greater degree of formality, the top of the fence can be covered with more horizontal pieces of bamboo, but this is not necessary in an informal setting, provided that the top of the fence is trimmed straight. The *kenninji* fence should not have any gaps between the vertical shafts of bamboo. It is used most often as a perimeter fence, but a short length of it is also useful as a way of defining separate areas within a garden.

The *kenninji* fence is sometimes mounted on a low stone wall. This combination is called a *ginkakuji* fence, and it is particularly imposing when set against a tall, pruned conifer hedge, as it is along the entrance path to the Silver Pavilion Temple in Kyoto, after which it is named. Sometimes, thinner types of bamboo are used for the vertical pieces, in which case the fence is known as the *shimizu* style. *Takeho* fences specifically use sheaves of bamboo branches instead, *kuromoji* fences use the branches of the Japanese spicebush (*Lindera umbellata*) and *hagi* fences are made with the slender branches of the Japanese bush clover (*Lespedeza* species). These brushwood or reed fences have a delightful rustic elegance about them, especially when the material is a different color from the bamboo; Japanese spicebush (*kuromoji*), for example, has rich reddish-brown bark. The straighter and more even in quality the brushwood is, the smoother the surface of the finished fence will be. Often this kind of fence looks as though it has been beautifully combed into place, though it is sometimes intentionally made with coarser material for an even more countrified look. While brushwood has an attractive

delicacy, the fence itself should look quite solid. Occasionally, the thinner material is used for the horizontal pieces instead; this style of fence draws people's attention to the thick canes of bamboo used

vertically, so it tends to emphasize the height of the fence rather than its length.

A popular way of using fences in Japan is not to take them from one end of a garden to the other, but to use them as a short screen or blind. The smallest gardens often have a high, narrow fence built at a right angle to the house, forming a sheltering windbreak near a doorway. These fences are called *sode-gaki*, or sleeve fences, and they are also useful for partly screening off sections of a garden. Any kind of weave, whether open or closed, formal or rustic, can be used for a sleeve fence, depending on its

above: *Branches of bamboo have been used to produce this sleeve fence (see also page 118). It is placed beside an entrance to screen part of the front of a building from view. Although rustic in style, it is tidy enough for a formal position. A huge cluster of bamboo branches decorates the end of the fence.*

facing page: *The kenninji fence (see also page 118) is the most common style of bamboo fence used for screening off areas around the house and garden.*

Constructing bamboo fences

method A

1

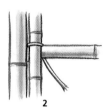

2

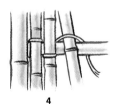

3

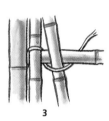

4

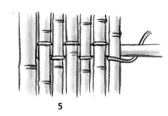

5

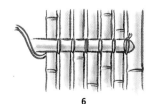

6

(seen from the back)

Kenninji **fences:** *Of the two methods for securing split bamboo along a horizontal strut with a continuous length of rope, (A) is less decorative, and the rope-work can later be hidden behind ornamental struts of halved canes of bamboo fastened to the fence, using the knot illustrated on the far right (C).*

The second method (B) produces an attractive pattern for kenninji-style fences (such as the one on page 116).

Brushwood fences: *This type of fence, shown on pages 115 and 117, is constructed by building up several rows of brushwood, held securely in place between horizontal struts of thin split bamboo. The brushwood is made to stand upright by tying the two horizontal struts together at regular intervals. First the back of the fence is constructed like this; then the horizontal struts are slightly loosened and another row of brushwood is inserted to create the front.*

Once a row is completed both back and front, halved canes of bamboo are clamped over the horizontal struts on either side of the fence. These canes are tightly fastened using individual, ornamental knots (C). The tips of the brushwood (which will be facing outwards on either side of the fence) are all neatly tucked into the fence. A beginner can use wire mesh to support the fence, but it is important to build up both sides of the fence so that the wire does not show.

method B

1

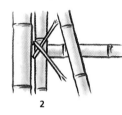

2

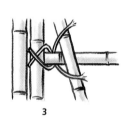

3

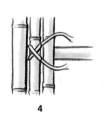

4

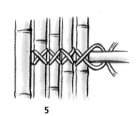

5

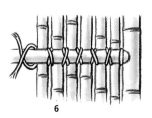

6

(seen from the back)

Yotsume **and** *teppo* **fences:** *The diagram on the right (C) shows the basic method for tying bamboo canes together for yotsume and teppo fences. Yotsume fences (shown on page 29 and 69, bottom right) have vertical canes which are arranged alternately on the front and back of the horizontal struts, which can be either three or four in number. Patterns can be created, for instance, using two vertical canes together at set intervals.*

Teppo fences (such as the one shown on page 54) are constructed in the same way, but with no space left between the vertical canes. Being screen fences, they are double the height of yotsume fences. Often they have alternating groups of five and three canes, the former placed in front of the horizontal struts and the latter behind.

The number of horizontal struts can differ according to the taste of the garden designer. They can be evenly spaced from top to bottom of the fence, or they can be divided into two groups of either two or three struts each. One group can be placed towards the top and the other towards the bottom of the fence, leaving the center of the fence clear and emphasizing its height.

method C

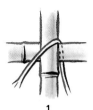

1

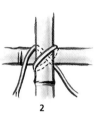

2

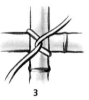

3

(seen from the back)

4

5

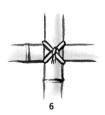

6

intended purpose and the general style of the garden. One famous kind, which is known as the *koetsuji* fence (named after yet another Kyoto temple), is long and narrow, and tapers towards the end in a distinctive curve. It is basically a *yarai*-style fence crowned with a thick sheaf of bamboo branches and thinly split bamboo. It is often used as a backdrop for a moss, rock and sand garden, separating this area from the rest of the surroundings. The *koetsuji* fence is effective when used against low-growing, formally pruned shrubs like azaleas, and ground-hugging plants.

The thicker and straighter the bamboo is, the more formal the fence will appear. Brushwood fences, on the other hand, can be constructed of locally available materials such as hazel, wattle or willow branches. Make friends with the people who coppice any nearby woods. Coarser, uneven branches can still be turned into a good fence with character, but it is important to remember that any one type of material used should all be of the same thickness and quality.

Garden walls in Japan were traditionally made of wattle and daub and were often whitewashed. Such walls serve as the background to some of the most famous Zen stone gardens, their whiteness mirroring the whiteness of the gravel. Pruned evergreens also look particularly fine silhouetted against a white wall. The choice of a fence or garden wall and the material of which it is made depends ultimately on the general formality of the entire garden. A rustic fence of brushwood may be suitable for part of a tea garden, while it would look too crude in an abstract Zen dry garden of rocks and sand. Some garden suppliers in the West stock woven wicker fences and screens made of split bamboo, heather, coppiced willow, reeds or other material. These may be too flimsy for most Japanese gardens, though it might be possible to give extra support to screens of this kind by adding horizontal struts of thick, straight

bamboo. The function of fences and walls in Japanese gardens is not simply to establish boundaries, for they help to draw the eye to the landscape beyond. The height of the fence should harmonize with plants both inside and outside the garden. Fences thus help to create a sense of space rather than that of confinement.

above: *An original bamboo screen design by Robert Ketchell and Eileen Tunnell for the "Ox-herding Pictures" Garden at the Hampton Court Flower Show in 1996.*

Borrowed vistas

This idea, of course, is by no means unique to Japanese gardens. If you have a garden that looks out towards a splendid distant vista, make the most of it by incorporating the view into the overall garden design. Don't hide it behind a dense hedge of Leyland cypress!

Fences, garden walls and hedges in Japanese gardens do not shut the garden in by shutting the external world out. Bamboo fences meant primarily for screening purposes are often built incorporating an open weave along the top to draw the eye to the landscape beyond. A rectilinear, dry Zen garden of the most austere kind is often surrounded by a whitewashed mud wall, which creates the feeling of an enclosed, self-sufficient world. But a row of majestic firs or cypresses beyond the garden wall not only helps to soften the stern line of the wall by drawing the eye upwards toward the sky; it also connects the garden with the vista that unfolds in the distance. At Entsu-ji Temple in Kyoto, columnar *hinoki* cypresses frame the distant view of Mount Hiei, grey like an ink painting on silk. A view of a shapely mountain is greatly esteemed in Japan for its spiritual and aesthetic resonance. At Shoden-ji Temple, also in Kyoto, the view of eastern mountains is echoed in the pruned azaleas in the dry garden.

In this way the garden is seen to mirror Nature and Nature seems to mirror the garden. This is the ultimate aim of the Japanese garden. It is a microcosm created to nestle within the macrocosm of the natural world, a segment of Nature as well as a work of art.

right: *The Max Koch Garden in Switzerland, designed by Anthony Paul, modifies the stone-slab type of foot-bridge to suit a location much more open than a typical Japanese landscape. Since there are few trees, the distant view of the mountains is not obscured and the feeling of wide open space is preserved. At the same time, the tall, stiff leaves of the water irises (*Iris laevigata*) and the flower spikes of the water plantain (*Alisma plantago-aquatica*) give a sense of height to the garden.*

CHAPTER THREE

Plant directory

The serenity of Japanese gardens comes from making careful designs seem utterly natural and unobtrusive. Clipped evergreens and pruned conifers serve as the backdrop for seasonal displays of fragile flowers. Japanese apricots and *Cornus officinalis* bloom in earliest spring. Azaleas such as *Rhododendron quinquefolium* and *R. reticulatum* create a haze of color at the height of spring, while summer brings the cool white blossoms of *Cornus kousa*, *Stewartia pseudocamellia*, or *Styrax japonicum*. A clump of "wild" flowers – balloon flowers, *Aster tartaricus* or toad lilies – signals the coming of autumn. The rustling of tall flower-heads of *Miscanthus sinensis* warns that frosts to redden the leaves of the maples will not be long. The bright red berries of *Ardisia crispa* decorate the garden through the cold winter months.

Understatement, rather than profusion, creates the calmness of this style of gardening.

Trees

Coniferous trees

Chamaecyparis pisifera (sawara cypress): drooping branches and scale-like leaves; hardy in zones 3 to 8; slow-growing; moist, non-alkaline soil in sun; *C. p.* "Filifera" (ito-hiba, hiyoku-hiba) has very fine foliage, and grows to 6 ft 6 in (2 m) in height; will not grow in shade.

Cryptomeria japonica (Japanese cedar; sugi): 81 x 20 ft (25 x 6 m); columnar in shape; hardy in zones 5 to 9; needs moisture and good drainage; sun; fast-growing; hates pollution; good as a background or screen; "Elegans Compacta" (6 ft 6 in (2 m) high) has green foliage that goes bronze in winter.

Juniperus chinensis "Kaizuka" (kaizuka-ibuki): 19 ft 6 in x 13 ft (6 x 4 m); hardy to zone 4; well-drained soil, preferably sandy; tolerates drought; sun; traditionally pruned gently by picking off soft tips by hand; cut back spurs shorter than outline of tree in autumn; tolerates pollution; dislikes root disturbance; suitable for planting in rows or as broad, pruned hedges.

Pinus densiflora (Japanese red pine; aka-matsu): 50 x 23 ft (15 x 7 m); conical, becoming flat-topped; hardy in zones 3 to 7; dry conditions; can be pruned; very intolerant of air pollution.

Pinus parviflora (Japanese white pine; goyo-matsu): conical; 32 ft 6 in x 26 ft (10 x 8 m); hardy in zones 4 to 7.

Pinus thunbergii (Japanese black pine; kuro-matsu): 49 x 19 ft 6 in (15 x 6 m); hardy in zones 5 to 7.

Podocarpus macrophyllus (yew pine; in US, southern or Japanese yew; kusa-maki, inu-maki): 49 x 19 ft 6 in (15 x 8 m); hardy in zones 8 to 10; conical with yew-like leaves; dislikes wet; fast-growing in warmer zones, needing summer humidity and heat to reach full height, otherwise it remains a shrub; can tolerate shade; *P. m.* var. *maki* (rakan-maki) is a much-prized Japanese variety with smaller leaves.

Sciadopitys verticillata (Japanese umbrella pine; koya-maki): 32 ft 6 in x 19 ft 6 in (10 x 6 m); hardy in zones 5 to 8; rich, moist, well-drained, neutral to slightly acid soil; full sun to partial shade; slow-growing and compact; peeling reddish bark; dislikes pollution; resents root disturbance; can be planted in groups.

Taxus cuspidata (Japanese yew; ichii, araragi, onko): 49 to 65 ft (15 to 20 m); hardy in zones 4 to 7; tolerates shade; needs moisture in autumn but dislikes wet; will not tolerate poor drainage; resents root disturbance; shelter from dry, cold winter winds; red fruits in autumn on female plants; peeling bark on older plants; prune twice a year in early summer and early autumn; old wood will not produce new buds; *Taxus cuspidata* var. *nana* (kyaraboku) is shorter and forms a round shape 6 ft 6 in to 13 ft (2 to 4 m); "Densa" is a shorter, female shrub 4 ft (1.2 m).

Thujopsis dolabrata (hiba arborvitae; asunaro, hiba); up to 49 ft (15 m); hardy to zone 5; conical; scale-like leaves; avoid strongly alkaline soils; likes moist, well-drained conditions; will not produce new shoots from branches more than three or four years old; start pruning early if a small shrub is wanted; prune at start of spring and autumn, picking off tips of shoots; "Nana" is a dwarf cultivar.

Torreya nucifera (Japanese nutmeg yew; kaya): 49 x 26 ft (15 x 8 m); hardy to zone 7; conical; sun or dappled shade; needs hot, humid summers to do well; good for south-eastern US, northern New Zealand, south-eastern Australia; good for moist riverside situations; shelter from wind; a hardy specimen tree.

Evergreen trees

Buxus microphylla var. *japonica* (Japanese box; tsuge): up to 16 ft 3 in (5 m); hardy to zone 5; half-shade; growth very slow; care needed in transplanting; likes lime; mulch to prevent shallow roots from drying out; wood used for making combs.

Castanopsis cuspidata (tsubura-jii): 26 x 26 ft (8 x 8 m); hardy to zone 5; spreading growth, drooping leaves; moist, rich, well-drained, slightly acid soil; sun; tolerates salt winds and pollution; for mass planting and broad, pruned hedges.

Cleyera japonica (sakaki): 10 x 10 ft (3 x 3 m); hardy to zone 5; rich, deep, acid soil; shade; can be pruned hard for broad hedges; use as underplanting; a tea-garden plant, also used around shrines.

Daphniphyllum macropodum (yuzuriha): to 49 ft (15 m); hardy to zone 6: a round shrub or tree; rich soil; half-shade; no pruning needed; leaves in whorls, which droop as new leaves appear; used for New Year's decorations; mass planting; suitable for north-facing gardens

Dendropanax trifidus (kakure-mino): 32 ft 6 in (10 m); hardy to zone 7; moist shade; very slow-growing; dislikes being pruned; resents root disturbance; suitable for north-facing gardens; used in shrines and tea gardens.

Euonymus japonicus (Japanese spindle; masaki): 13 to 16 ft (4 to 5 m); hardy to zones 7 to 9; sun, partial shade or shade; vigorous, bushy; tolerates pollution, poorer soils and alkaline conditions; can be pruned; suitable for hedges, underplanting; some varieties are variegated.

Ilex crenata (box-leaved holly, Japanese holly; inu-tsuge): 16 ft 3 in x 13 ft (5 x 4 m); hardy to zones 5 to 7; small, round, glossy leaves; partial shade; moist conditions; important for topiary in Japan; slow-growing but vigorous; avoid winter wind; if soil is alkaline, give an annual feed of acid fertilizer.

Ilex integra (mochi-no-ki): 23 to 26 ft (7 to 8 m); hardy to zones 7 to 9; moist, rich soil; sun; slow-growing; prune heavily in early summer by trimming back branches to two or three new leaves; can be transplanted even when quite big; used near shrines.

Ilex rotunda (kurogane-mochi): 32 ft 6 in to 49 ft (10 to 15 m); hardy to zone 7 only; tolerates half-shade; slow-growing; red berries in winter.

Lithocarpus edulis (matebashii): 32 ft 6 in (10 m); hardy to zone 6; sun or partial shade; fast-growing; tolerates heavy pruning; for hedging or mass planting.

Osmanthus x fortunei (hiiragi-mokusei: *O. fragrans* x *O. heterophyllus*): 16 ft 3 in (5 m); hardy to zone 6; upright; holly-like, glossy green leaves; half-shade or complete shade; prune; tolerant of sea air; suitable for hedges and planting in rows; fragrant tubular white flowers in late summer to autumn; likes slightly acid soil.

Osmanthus heterophyllus (Chinese holly; hiiragi): 13 to 26 ft (4 to 8 m); hardy in zones 7 to 9; holly-like, spiny, leathery leaves; tolerates shade; slowly forms a dense round shrub; can be pruned; tolerates sea air; can be grown alone, but also suitable for hedges; fragrant, white tubular flowers on female plants in late autumn, berries mature by the following summer.

Quercus myrsinifolia (shira-kashi): up to 65 ft (20 m) tall; hardy to zone 6; clay soil; tolerates half-shade; takes heavy pruning; will not tolerate pollution; tolerates sea air; can be used as a windbreak; plant alone, or as hedging, or in a row.

Ternstroemia gymnanthera (mokkoku): 16 to 32 ft 6 in (5 to 10 m); usually dislikes temperatures below -5°C/23°F; ripe wood bears colder conditions; partial or complete shade; rich acid soil; in early summer remove the longest central stem from each new growth.

facing page, from top left:

Japanese spindle (Euonymus japonicus)
Acer japonicum in October at Westonbirt Arboretum, Gloucestershire
Fatsia japonica
Crape myrtle (Lagerstroemia indica)

Deciduous trees

Acer japonicum (full moon maple; ha-uchiwa-kaede): hardy to zone 5; tolerant of partial shade; slow-growing; acid soil; dislikes salt air; rounded leaves, seven to thirteen shallowly toothed lobes, turning yellow and red in autumn; better than *A. palmatum* in heavy or alkaline soils.

Acer palmatum (iroha-momiji, takao-kaede, momiji): many variations in leaf shape and color which can change from spring through to autumn; hardy to zone 5 if protected in winter; vulnerable to early spring frosts; rich, deep, acid soil that does not dry out; sun (but some paler varieties may be scorched in hot sun); do not prune tips of branches; cut back overlong spurs and crowded branches at base; if the size of the plant needs to be reduced, cut back long branches to the next fork; has a very short dormant period so prune in late autumn, early winter; good for planting by edge of ponds and near lanterns; mulch with leaf mould in autumn and early spring; *A. p.* var. *heptalobum* has leaves with between five and seven lobes, turning a rich orange and red color in the autumn; *A. p.* var. *matsumurae* (yama-momiji) has bigger leaves which are toothed; "Osaka-zuki" has a classical seven-lobed leaf-shape and orange-red autumn color; "Sango-kaku" produces vibrant yellow autumn leaves and brilliant red branches which look lacquered; "Shindeshojo" and "Beni-tsukasa" also have very good leaf shapes; the "Dissectum" group has deeply divided, frond-like leaves.

Cercidiphyllum japonicum (katsura): to 81 ft (25 m); hardy in zones 6 to 8; moist, rich, neutral to acid soil; sun, half-shade; fast-growing but dislikes pruning; pyramidal; no pests; brilliant scarlet autumn color (best in acid soil); var. *magnificum* shorter (to 32 ft 6 in (10 m)) with larger leaves; f. *pendulum* has a weeping habit.

Clerodendrum trichotomum (kusagi): moderate to very hardy deciduous small tree (16 ft (5 m)); hardy to zone 7; produces striking bright blue berries with crimson calyces in the autumn.

Euonymus hamiltonianus subsp. *sieboldianus* (spindle tree; mayumi): 16 ft (5 m); hardy to zone 4; fast-growing; sun; four-lobed pinkish-red fruits split to reveal red seeds on female plants in autumn; pruning not necessary but can be done during the winter to keep a natural shape, removing long or weak branches or suckers at base; flowers form on short branches; autumn color.

Ginkgo biloba (maidenhair tree; icho): to 97 ft (30 m); hardy to zone 3; upright; slow-growing; needs sun; flat, fan-like leaves turn brilliant yellow in autumn; tolerates drought and pollution; dioecious; trees grown in West tend to be male, but in Japan the nuts are eaten.

Poncirus trifoliata (trifoliate orange, Japanese bitter orange; karatachi): 6 ft 6 in to 10 ft (2 to 3 m); hardy to zone 6; tolerant of partial shade, but prefers sun; dislikes root disturbance; fragrant five-petalled flowers in spring before leaves; inedible fruit like small oranges; very sharp spines on branches; used for tall, thick hedges.

Sophora japonica (Japanese pagoda tree; enju): 32 ft 6 in to 81 ft (10 to 25 m); hardy in zones 4 to 8; full sun; deep, rich soil, but tolerates poorer conditions; a spreading, round tree; pinnate leaves; creamy flowers in late summer; can be pruned; can be planted in groups; traditionally an auspicious plant.

Sorbus commixta (Japanese rowan: nana-kamado): 32 ft 6 in to 49 ft (10 to 15 m); hardy to zone 5; tolerates partial shade; rather dislikes root disturbance; slow-growing; autumn color and berries.

Zelkova serrata (keaki; keyaki): to 65 ft (20 m); hardy to zone 6; sun but tolerates partial shade; deep, rich but well-drained soil; deep roots; can be transplanted as a fully grown tree; forms a round shape but does not have a tall central trunk; tolerates hard pruning in winter, though this is not necessary except to maintain a good overall shape; attractive autumn color; withstands wind, but dislikes air pollution, drought, heat from pavement and roads.

Flowering trees

Camellia japonica (common camellia; yabu-tsubaki): 29 x 26 ft (9 x 8 m); hardy in zones 7 to 9; spreading or upright evergreen shrub or tree; sun; red single flowers with golden trumpet-shaped stamens in late winter, early spring; glossy dark green leaves; rich acid soil; do not prune; for growing on its own or for hedging; widely grown in Japan; *C. j.* var. *hortensis* (tsubaki) includes garden cultivars, which are pruned, often into a tall column; after flowering cut back branches to a healthy bud, keeping in mind the overall shape of the bush; protect plant with mulch against drying out during winter; hybrids appreciate partial shade and need protection against cold winds and late frosts; "Shiro Wabisuke" is a round shrub; small, elegant flowers in midwinter, early spring.

Camellia sasanqua (sazanka): 19 ft 6 in x 10 ft (6 x 3 m); hardy in zones 7 to 9; evergreen columnar shrub or tree; rich, deep, acid soil; tolerates shade and pollution; dislikes pruning; good as a wind-break; single flowers silky and informal; flowers earlier than common camellia, during the winter in Japan, may bloom in late autumn in some climates; prune as for *Camellia* hybrids after flowering; protect plant against summer drought.

Cercis chinensis (Chinese redbud; hanazuo): 6 ft 6 in to 16 ft (2 to 5 m); hardy to zone 6; a deciduous, dense shrub; sun; dark pink flowers in spring before leaves; few pests; resents transplanting when older.

Cornus kousa (yamaboshi): 32 ft 6 in (10 m); hardy in zones 5 to 8; a conical, deciduous tree; sun (but young trees dislike strong summer sun) or partial shade; acid soil; vigorous; tolerates drought; flowers surrounded by four handsome pointed creamy-white bracts produced in early summer, followed by red fruit; dislikes pruning.

Cornus officinalis (sanshuyu): a spreading deciduous shrub; clusters of tiny yellow flowers early in spring; mix with pink *Prunus mume*.

Hamamelis japonica (Japanese witch hazel; mansaku): 16 ft 3 in to 32 ft 6 in (5 to 10 m); hardy to zone 6; a shapely deciduous tree; sun but tolerates partial shade; appreciates slightly acid soil; delicately scented yellow or orange ribbon-like flowers in late winter; autumn color; *H. mollis* (Chinese witch hazel) is more common in the West; *H.* x *intermedia* varieties are hybrids of *H. mollis* and *H. japonica*.

Lagerstroemia indica (crape myrtle; saru-suberi): 13 to 16 ft 3 in (4 to 5 m); hardy in zone 9; sun; deciduous; long whippy branches; flowers in summer; for larger flowers prune branches back to 4 to 8 in (10 to 20 cm) in winter when dormant.

Magnolia hypoleuca (ho-no-ki): 65 to 97 ft (20 to 30 m); hardy to zone 5; fragrant yellow flowers 8 in (20 cm) in diameter, with prominent stamens in spring; fragrant leaves; deciduous.

Magnolia kobus (kobushi): 32 ft 6 in to 49 ft (10 to 15 m); hardy to zone 4; fragrant white flowers in spring before leaves; dislikes root disturbance; tolerant of partial shade and moist, alkaline soil; fragrant leaves; *M. kobus* and *M. liliiflora* will grow tall; stop top growth when desired height is reached; placing a rock under the roots of the tree will encourage roots and branches to spread.

Magnolia liliiflora (shi-mokuren): deciduous; reddish-purple goblet flowers; "Nigra" is shorter (to 8 ft (2.5 m)) with purple-red flowers.

Magnolia salicifolia (Japanese willow-leaved magnolia; tamu-shiba): hardy to zone 5; white blossoms in early spring; deciduous leaves have an aniseed scent when crushed; moist, acid conditions; sun or partial shade; closely related to *M. kobus*.

Magnolia sieboldii (oyama-renge): 13 to 16 ft 3 in (4 to 5 m); hardy to zone 7; creamy, slightly nodding flowers with prominent purplish-red anthers and a fruity scent in late spring, early summer; used for flower arrangements at tea ceremonies; tolerant of moist, alkaline soil; deciduous.

Magnolia stellata (shide-kobushi): 13 to 16 ft 3 in (4 to 5 m); hardy in zones 3 to 8; grows fast

facing page, from top left:
Euonymus alatus *in October*
Hydrangea macrophylla *"Normalis" in August*
Ardisia crispa *(syn.* A. crenata*) "Coral Berry"*
Saxifraga stolonifera *in October*

in full sun; white fragrant flowers with twelve to eighteen ribbon-like petals in early spring before leaves; rich deep soil; tolerant of alkaline conditions; deciduous.

Magnolia wieseneri (M. hypoleuca x M. sieboldii): 19 ft 6 in x 16 ft 3 in (6 x 5 m); hardy to zone 7; heavily scented pendulous white flowers with bright red anthers; deciduous.

Prunus incisa (Fuji cherry; mame-zakura, fuji-zakura): a small wild cherry growing about 9 ft 9 in (3 m) tall; hardy to zone 5; single, white to pale pink flowers in early spring.

Prunus jamasakura (Japanese hill cherry; yama-zakura): a wild cherry to 19 ft 6 in (6 m) tall; hardy to zones 5 and 6; young leaves are bronze-colored; small, pinkish-white flowers; much admired in Japan over the centuries; a parent of hybrid Japanese cherries.

Prunus mume (Japanese plum, Japanese apricot; ume): 5 ft 6 in to 32 ft 6 in (2 to 10 m); hardy to zone 6; rich but sandy soil; sun; delicately scented flowers with five white round petals produced in early spring before cherries; yellow fruit in summer; there are cultivars with double flowers, also in shades of pink; reduce branches with flower buds by a third and prune back long spurs with no buds in winter, after the round flower-buds appear; one of the most important flowering trees in Japan; green fruit used for pickles and cordials; "Pendula" (to 19ft 6 in (6 m) tall) is a weeping form with pink flowers.

Prunus Sato-zakura Group (Japanese flowering cherries; sakura): hardy to zone 4; most are derived from P. serrulata; prone to infection after pruning; choose small or dwarf varieties if space is limited.

Prunus subhirtella (winter-flowering cherry; higan cherry; higan-zakura): 26 x 26 ft (8 x 8 m); hardy to zone 4; clusters of pink or white flowers produced from autumn to spring; "Pendula Rosea" has weeping branches and rosy flowers.

Prunus x yedoensis (yoshino cherry; somei-yoshino); hardy in zones 5 to 8; spreading, arching growth; a weeping form is available.

Stewartia pseudocamellia (natsu-tsubaki, shara-no-ki): up to 32 ft 6 in (10 m); hardy in zones 5 to 8; columnar; rich neutral to acid soil; avoid root disturbance; sun, but hates dry conditions; do not prune; white camellia-like flowers in early summer; autumn leaf color and mottled bark; deciduous; shelter against winter winds; S. monadelpha is smaller.

Styrax japonicum (Japanese snowbell; ego-no-ki): 23 to 26 ft (7 to 8 m); hardy to zone 5; deciduous; sun but tolerates partial shade; rich, slightly acid soil; water well while settling in; white pendulous flowers like snowdrops in early summer; berries poisonous; do not prune; can be planted in rows in an informal shrubbery.

Shrubs

Evergreen shrubs

Ardisia japonica (marlberry; yabu-koji): 4 to 6 in (10 to 15 cm); hardy in zones 6 to 9; shady, moist, well-drained conditions; small, leathery leaves and red berries; prune close to the ground in early spring; use for underplanting.

Aucuba japonica (spotted laurel; aoki): 3 ft 3 in to 6 ft 6 in (1 to 2 m); hardy to zone 6, but may survive colder temperatures if sheltered; rich, moist soil in shade; a round shrub; avoid pruning except to remove old branches at ground level; tolerates pollution; suitable for north-facing gardens, tea gardens, for underplanting; red berries on female plants during winter.

Eurya emarginata (hama-hi-sakaki): 5 ft (1.5 m); half-hardy to zone 9: glossy leaves tinged red during the winter; partial shade; vigorous; prune; tolerates salt wind; for hedging.

Eurya japonica (hi-sakaki): 16 ft 3 in (5 m); hardy to zone 8; partial or complete shade; rather slow growth; dry soil; used as hedging around tea gardens; also broad, pruned hedges; flowers smell rather unpleasant.

Fatsia japonica (yatsude): 6 ft 6 in to 9 ft 9 in (2 to 3 m); hardy in zones 8 to 10, with lower temperatures tolerated if sheltered; moist rich soil; sun or dappled shade, full shade in a sheltered position; deeply lobed leathery leaves; no pruning; flowers in winter; suitable for solitary or group planting, underplanting.

Juniperus chinensis var. *procumbens* (hai-byakushin): 2 ft 6 in x 6 ft 6 in (75 cm x 2 m); hardy in zones 8 to 10; sun; dry sandy soil especially if alkaline; no pruning; dislikes root disturbance; "Nana" grows to 1 ft (30 cm) tall.

Mahonia japonica (hiiragi-nanten): 5 ft to 6 ft 6 in (1.5 to 2 m); hardy to zone 6; partial or complete shade; best in acid soils; fast-growing and upright; no pruning; fragrant yellow flowers in midwinter.

Photinia glabra (Chinese hawthorn; kaname-mochi): 9 ft 9 in x 9 ft 9 in (3 x 3 m); hardy to zones 7 and 8, but lower temperatures tolerated if sheltered; sun to partial shade; avoid excessive wet; dense, round growth; attractive red young leaves; good for broad, pruned hedges; prune four times through spring to summer for fresh leaf-buds, but do not prune heavily in autumn; "Rubens" has particularly fine young red leaves.

Pieris japonica (Japanese andromeda; asebi): 6 ft 6 in to 16 ft 3 in (2 to 5 m); hardy in zones 5 to 8; rich, acid soil; partial shade, but also tolerates full sun; tolerates alkaline soils; protect from winter winds; a round bush; white flowers in late winter and spring; new panicles form in August; remove any forming earlier; leaves poisonous if eaten.

Deciduous shrubs

Berberis thunbergii (Japanese barberry; megi); 3 ft 3 in (1 m); hardy in zones 4 to 8; a round shrub; leaves change color in autumn; use for hedging; f. *atropurpurea* has purple-red or purple-bronze foliage; needs sun for good color.

Euonymus alatus (winged euonymus; nishikigi): 6 ft 6 in (2 m); hardy to zone 3; dense and bushy; dryish soil; sun, but tolerates partial shade; can be pruned hard; crimson leaves in autumn; "Compactus" is shorter and more dense in growth.

Ilex serrata (Japanese winterberry; ume-modoki): 9 ft 9 in (3 m); hardy to zone 3; sun; slow-growing but bushy with purple stems; female trees produce red berries, appreciated by birds in winter; bright pink flowers in spring; pruning not necessary except to reduce long spurs.

Salix babylonica (weeping willow; shidare-yanagi): 39 ft (12 m); hardy in zones 6 to 8, but shelter against cold and winter winds; moist but well-drained soil; good for waterside; sun; S. x sepulcralis "Chrysocoma" (golden weeping willow) has slender yellow shoots.

Salix gracilistyla (rosegold pussy willow; neko-yanagi): 1 ft 8 in to 9ft 9 in (50 cm to 3 m); hardy to zone 6; a waterside willow with male and female plants; fluffy grey catkins.

Zanthoxylum piperitum (Japanese pepper; sansho): to 7 ft 4 in (2.5 m); thorny and deciduous; leaves aromatic when crushed; leaves and seeds used in cooking.

Flowering shrubs

Corylopsis pauciflora (buttercup witch hazel; hyuga-mizuki): 5 x 8 ft (1.5 x 2.5 m); hardy to zone 6; acid soil in sun or partial shade; racemes of pale yellow flowers in spring; deciduous.

Daphne odora (jinchoge): 5 ft (1.5 m); hardy in zones 7 to 9; evergreen; moist, light, acid soil; sun or partial shade; dislikes root disturbance; often pruned to a sphere; cut back branches immediately after flowering; dislikes dry conditions and poor drainage; "Aureomarginata" is more hardy.

Deutzia gracilis (Japanese snowflower; hime-utsugi): hardy to zone 4; smaller than D. crenata; bushy and upright to 3 ft 3 in (1 m); white flowers in late spring, early summer; good by waterside.

Enkianthus campanulatus (sarasa-dodan): 13 x

facing page, from top left:
Miscanthus sinensis *with a dwarf Alberta spruce (*Picea glauca *"Conica")*
Fargesia murieliae *"Simba" (design by Natural & Oriental Water Gardens, Hampton Court Flower Show, 1998)*
Sagina *in a rock garden*
Cycas revoluta

13 ft (4 x 4 m); hardy to zone 7; has creamy-yellow bell-like flowers streaked with red.

Enkianthus cernuus f. *rubens* (beni-dodan): hardy to zone 5; nodding, red, urn-shaped flowers.

Enkianthus perulatus (dodan-tsutsuji): 3 ft 3 in to 6 ft 6 in (1 to 2 m); hardy in zones 5 to 7, but shelter against cold in winter; sun; well-drained acid soil; slow-growing; deciduous; grown for its white, bell-shaped flowers (spring) and autumn leaf color; tolerates hard pruning immediately after flowering; if its shape is more important than its flowers, prune in winter.

Hydrangea macrophylla (lacecap and hortensia hydrangeas; ajisai): 5 to 6 ft 6 in (1.5 to 2 m); hardy to zone 5; moist rich soil; acid soil with a pH reading of less than 5.5 will produce blue flowers, a pH reading greater than 5.5 will produce pink flowers; white-flowering varieties not affected; tolerates shade; prune back flowering branches to the next non-flowering branch immediately after flowering; useful in north-facing gardens or for interplanting between trees.

Hydrangea paniculata (nori-utsugi): 9 ft 9 in (3 m); hardy to zone 3; partial shade; fast-growing; takes pruning; for underplanting.

Kerria japonica (yamabuki): 6 ft 6 in x 8 ft (2 x 2.5 m); hardy in zones 4 to 9; moist, rich soil; sun or partial shade; yellow single or double flowers in spring; pruning not required unless the plant is too big; remove non-flowering, dead and weak branches at base; good for planting in groups.

Lespedeza bicolor (Japanese bush clover; yama-hagi): 5 to 6 ft 6 in (1.5 to 2 m); hardy to zone 5; sun; good in groups; rich soil; tiny purple-pink flowers at the end of summer and in autumn; weeping branches; prune if necessary after leaf-fall; cut back old branches to the ground and reduce younger branches by half; *L. thunbergii*: a subshrub; cut back branches to within 4 in (10 cm) of the ground; cv. "Albiflora" has white flowers; cv. "Versicolor" has white and rosy purple flowers on the same plant.

Osmanthus fragrans f. *aurantiacus* (fragrant olive, sweet tea; kin-mokusei): to 32 ft 6 in (10 m); half-hardy to zone 8; clusters of tiny orange blooms with an intense fruity scent in autumn; prune into a column; when growing from a sapling, stop top growth; cut back long branches in winter to prune into the desired shape; allow it to become slightly bigger each year to encourage buds on new growth.

Paeonia suffruticosa (tree peony; moutan; botan): to 6 ft 6 in (2 m); hardy to zone 6; a deciduous shrub; sun; shallow roots; resents strong afternoon sunlight and dry conditions; humus-rich soil; resents root disturbance; many cultivars; prune down to one or two flowering buds in late autumn.

Rhaphiolepis umbellata (sharinbai): 6 ft 6 in (2 m); hardy in zone 9, but lower temperatures tolerated in shelter; sun; good near the sea; rich soil; bushy

evergreen; white flowers, sometimes tinted pink, in round racemes in early summer; tea gardens; cv. "Minor" is a dwarf cultivar.

[*Rhododendron*] *Shakunage* refers to evergreen rhododendrons with big leathery leaves; to 13 ft (4 m) in height; rich, well-drained, acid soil in half-shade; slow-growing; they dislike pruning and root disturbance.

[*Rhododendron*] *Tsutsuji*: azaleas flowering in spring, early summer; satsuki- and kurume-tsutsuji (satsuki and kurume hybrid azaleas) both semi-evergreen, short (1 ft 8 in to 3 ft 3 in (50 cm to 1 m) in height), vigorous and suitable for hard pruning; excellent for group planting and broad, pruned hedges; prune when the last flowers are still on the bush; to reduce the size of a plant that has become too large, cut back half the branches to a size smaller than the desired one; the following year prune back the rest of the branches.

R. quinquefolium (shiro-yashio, goyo-tsutsuji), *R. reticulatum* (mitsuba-tsutsuji) and *R. japonicum* (renge-tsutsuji): deciduous azaleas; not vigorous; should be tidied only if necessary to remove weak, dead or crossed branches immediately after flowering; *R. quinquefolium* is a delicate small tree; white flowers with green speckles among leaves produced in whorls of five; frost hardy to zone 6, but protect it.

Spiraea cantoniensis (Reeves's spiraea; kodemari): 3 ft 3 in to 6 ft 6 in (1 to 2 m); hardy in zones 6 to 9; a deciduous or semi-evergreen shrub; flowers mid-spring; rich soil; sun; fast-growing; can be pruned into a sphere; prune after flowering, cutting back to an upward-turning bud; every three years cut back old branches to fresh young growth at the base of the plant.

Spiraea thunbergii (yuki-yanagi): 3 ft 3 in to 5 ft (1 to 1.5 m); hardy to zone 3; flowers in early spring; sun: trailing branches; prune in the same way as *S. cantoniensis*.

Viburnum japonicum (hakusanboku): to 6 ft (1.8 m); hardy to zone 6; round, evergreen shrub; small, fragrant, white flowers in round cymes in early summer; sun; grows fast; takes hard pruning.

Viburnum plicatum f. *plicatum* (Japanese snowball; odemari): to 9 ft 9 in (3 m); hardy in zones 5 to 8; low-growing, deciduous shrub; lacecap flowers in late summer; sun; slow growth; light pruning; good as a specimen plant for a front garden.

Berries

Ardisia crispa (manryo): 2 ft to 3 ft 3 in (60 cm to 1 m); half-hardy, but can survive temperatures down to -18°C/0°F if sheltered; evergreen; partial shade; berries from winter to spring below leaves growing from the top of the plant; cut back stem every four or five years in spring to reduce height.

Callicarpa japonica (Japanese beauty-berry; murasaki-shikibu): 9 ft 9 in to 16 ft 3 in (3 to 5 m); hardy in zones 6 to 8; sun; deciduous; can be pruned close to the ground in the late autumn or early spring, but do not prune the tips of branches; stems die back to the ground in cold areas; purple berries in autumn; for informal shrubbery; named after Murasaki-shikibu, author of *The Tale of Genji*; *C. dichotoma* (ko-murasaki) is smaller.

Sarcandra glabra (senryo): 2 to 3 ft (60 cm to 90 cm); hardy to zone 8, but shelter in winter and mulch; evergreen; grown for red winter berries; partial shade; use for underplanting; do not let leaves burn in hot sun; fast growth; tolerant of sea air; hates dry conditions; if a bigger plant is desired, reduce branches to a leaf node in late winter; often grown with *Ardisia crispa* (manryo).

Nandina domestica (heavenly bamboo; nanten): 5 ft to 6 ft 6 in (1.5 to 3 m), but some cultivars are shorter; half-hardy in zones 7 to 9; sun or partial shade; evergreen or semi-evergreen; red berries in winter months; dark purple-green leaves; planted under eaves of houses – not, as E. A. Bowles (1865–1954), the English horticulturalist, suggested, because the wood was used as tooth-picks, but to prevent the flowers being splashed by rain; replant in autumn and mulch; remove old and dead branches in early spring, and cut back tips of stems for branching shape; an auspicious plant.

Ground-cover

Ophiopogon japonicus (Japanese snake's beard, mondo grass; ryu-no-hige, ja-no-hige): 4 to 12 in (10 to 30 cm); hardy to zone 7; prefers moist, slightly acid conditions and shade; top-dress with leaf mould in autumn; flower-spikes in summer; strap-like narrow leaves 4 to 8 in (10 to 20 cm); forms dense ground-cover; tolerates low light (good under eaves to prevent mud splashing); *O. planiscapus* "Nigrescens" has black leaves, lilac flowers, followed by blue berries, and is hardy; *O. jaburan* (noshi-ran) has striped variegated forms, and is hardy.

Reineckea carnea (kichijo-so): 3 ¼ to 7 ¼ in (8 to 18 cm) tall; hardy to zone 7; neutral to acid soil; partial shade; evergreen, good for ground-cover; blooms in late autumn.

Saxifraga stolonifera (yuki-no-shita): 8 in to 1 ft

facing page, from top left:
Farfugium japonicum (*syn.* Ligularia tussilaginea)
Begonia grandis *ssp.* evansiana *in October*
Chinese lantern (Physalis alkekengi) *in the autumn*
Liriope muscari *in October*

8 in (20 to 50 cm); hardy to zone 4; evergreen perennial, with thick, kidney-shaped leaves, purplish underneath with white veins; white flowers in late spring to early summer; prefers wet, shady, rocky places; requires very little soil.

Grasses and Bamboos

Grasses

Carex hachijoensis "Evergold" (hachijokan-suge): 1 ft x 1 ft 2 in (30 x 35 cm); hardy to zone 4; a creamy yellow and green, variegated variety of a tufted, evergreen sedge; moist well-drained conditions in sun or partial shade.

Hakonechloa macra "Aureola" (uraha-gusa): 1 ft 2 ½ in x 1 ft 4 in (36 x 40 cm); hardy to zone 4; a variegated form of a deciduous, clump-forming, perennial grass; bright gold with green stripes, red-tinted in the autumn; moist soil, partial shade for good color.

Imperata cylindrica "Rubra" (Japanese blood-grass, chigaya): hardy to zone 9; a perennial grass forming loose clumps; leaves to 1 ft 8 in (50 cm) long, tips turning blood-red.

Miscanthus sinensis (Chinese silvergrass; susuki): 3 ft 3 in to 6 ft 6 in (1 to 2 m); hardy to zone 5; a clump-forming, upright grass with silvery plume-like flower-heads in late summer to autumn; cut away old leaves late in winter; grows naturally on disturbed land; dislikes winter wet, but tolerates a reasonably moist site.

Bamboos

Bambusa multiplex (hedge bamboo): 9 ft 9 in to 16 ft 3 in (3 to 5 m); hardy in zone 8; shoots appear from summer into autumn.

Chimonobambusa marmorea (kan-chiku): up to 9 ft 9 in (3 m); hardy to zone 5; shade; for hedging; likes a warm climate; rich soil; a bamboo with solid (not hollow) stems and red, mottled canes.

Chimonobambusa quadrangularis (shiho-chiku): 16 ft 3 in to 19 ft 6 in (5 to 6 m); canes flattened on all four sides; shoots produced in the autumn and winter; shade; rich soil; difficult to transplant; good for small courtyard gardens; prefers warmer climates.

Hibanobambusa tranquillans (inyo-chiku): 9 ft 9 in to 16 ft 3 in (3 to 5 m); hardy to zone 7; a hardy hybrid of *Sasa* and *Phyllostachys*; large leaves and smooth bamboo-like canes; used for hedges; tolerates drought.

Phyllostachys bambusoides (ma-dake): 32 ft 6 in to 65 ft (10 to 20 m); hardy to zone 8; sun; rich soil in warmer climates; difficult to transplant; for bamboo groves; harvested for fencing and crafts; "Castillonis" (kimmei-chiku): 26 ft to 32 ft 6 in (8 to 10 m); hardy; golden-yellow stalks and green leaves marked in creamy-white or yellow.

Phyllostachys edulis (moso-dake): 49 to 65 ft (15 to 20 m); hardy to zone 8; the thickest bamboo; used for bamboo groves; shoots eaten; difficult to transplant.

Phyllostachys nigra (kuro-chiku): 6 ft 6 in to 9 ft 9 in (2 to 3 m); hardy to zone 6 but dies back in winter in cold areas; canes are dark green the first year, turning black from the second; shade; for a small courtyard garden or as background.

Phyllostachys pubescens f. *heterocycla* (kikko-chiku): hardy to zone 7; joints zig-zag up the canes which bulge between the joints; an unusual and rare ornamental bamboo.

Phyllostachys sulphurea (ogon-ko-chiku): to 26 ft (8 m); hardy to zone 6; green canes turn bright yellow streaked with green.

Pleioblastus simonii (me-dake): 6 ft 6 in to 13 ft (2 to 4 m); hardy to zone 6; good for planting near rivers.

Semiarundinaria kagamiana (rikuchu-dake): 9 ft 9 in to 16 ft 3 in (3 to 5 m); hardy to zone 7; bushy; tolerates both sun and shade.

Semiarundinaria yashadake "Kimmei": hardy to zone 8; yellow canes tinted pink and green, turning dusky red in sunlight during their first winter.

Sinobambusa tootsik (to-chiku): hardy only to zone 9; usually pruned; stop top when 9 ft 9 in to 26 ft (3 to 8 m) in height; side shoots selected for round leaf growth, all other side shoots removed.

Shorter bamboo grasses

Pleioblastus auricoma (kamuro-zasa): 1 ft to 5 ft (30 cm to 1.5 m); hardy to zone 7; gold and green variegated leaves; likes shade.

Pleioblastus variegatus (chigo-zasa, shima-dake); 1 ft to 3 ft 3 in (30 cm to 1 m); hardy to zone 7; makes a thick and bushy clump; green and cream variegated leaves.

Sasa tsuboïana (ibuki-zasa): 5 ft to 6 ft 6 in (1.5 to 2 m); hardy to zone 5; forms round clumps with dark green leaves.

Sasa veitchii (kuma-zasa): to 3 ft (90 cm); hardy to zone 6; for dense ground-cover; coarse leaves.

Shibataea kumasasa (okame-zasa): 3 ft 3 in to 6 ft 6 in (1 to 2 m); hardy to zone 6; shade; for ground-cover or wide, pruned hedges.

Mosses

Mosses used in Japan

Mosses need an acid, moist but well-drained environment. Transplant them early in spring.

Conocephalum conicum (ja-goke), *Marchantia polymorpha* (zeni-goke), *Pogonatum contortum* (niwa-sugi-goke), *P. grandifolium* (seitaka-sugi-goke), *Polytrichum commune* (haircap moss; sugi-goke), *Selaginella japonica* (eizan-goke), *Steroden plumaeformis* (mukumuku-chirimen-goke).

Alternatives

Arenaria tetraquetra: hardy to zone 7; forms a dense evergreen mat; star-shaped white flowers in the spring.

Sagina subulata (Irish moss, Corsican pearlwort): hardy to zone 2; evergreen mats 4 in (10 cm) high.

Selaginella kraussiana (Krauss's spikemoss): hardy only to zone 8; an evergreen, South African perennial that forms a dense mat.

Ferns

Adiantum aleuticum (Aleutian maidenhair fern; kujaku-shida): 2 ft 6 in x 2 ft 6 in (75 x 75 cm); hardy to zone 2; deciduous or semi-evergreen; thought to look like the plumes of a peacock tail.

Blechnum nipponicum (shishigashira, iwashi-bone, mukade-gusa): hardy only to zone 9; an evergreen fern; partial or full shade; moist acid soil; upright leathery fronds, likened to a lion's mane, centipedes, or the backbone of a sardine.

Cyrtomium macrophyllum (hiroha-yabu-sotetsu): 1 ft 6 in x 2 ft (45 x 60 cm); hardy to zone 7; evergreen, large-leaved holly fern; also *C. fortunei* (yabu-sotetsu), hardy to zone 8, and *C. falcatum* (oni-yabu-sotetsu), semi-evergreen or deciduous in colder places, hardy to zone 9, needing shelter.

Davallia mariesii (hare's foot fern; shinobu); 6 in (15 cm) in height; hardy only to zone 9; deciduous; finely cut fronds.

Dryopteris erythrosora (Japanese red shield fern, painted fern; beni-shida): hardy to zone 8; a deciduous fern growing from reddish shoots; *Athyrium nipponicum*, hardy to zone 4, also grows from a red root-stock and has purple-tinted, green fronds; both need moisture in shade; neutral to acid soil; mulch well when planting.

Equisetum hiemale (tokusa): hardy to zone 5; an evergreen fern; grown for upright stalks to 1 ft 8 in (50 cm); good for planting around water basins.

Matteuccia struthiopteris (ostrich fern, kusa-sotetsu): hardy to zone 1; deciduous with upright fronds.

Polystichum polyblepharum (Japanese tassel fern; inode): 2 to 3 ft (60 to 90 cm); hardy to zone 5; an evergreen fern with shuttlecock fronds.

Selaginella tamariscina (iwa-hiba): hardy to zone 6; an evergreen perennial with a long stalk and scaly leaves; grows on rocky terrain; likes moderately rich, moist, well-drained, neutral to slightly acid soil, and partial shade.

facing page, from top left:
Double day lily (Hemerocallis fulva) *in July.*
White water lily (Nymphaea alba)
Sacred lotus (Nelumbo nucifera)
Iris ensata

Tropical Specimen Plants

Cycas revoluta (Japanese sago palm, Japan fern palm; sotetsu): 9 ft 9 in to 26 ft (3 to 8 m); hardy only to zone 9; full sun; in early summer when new leaves have emerged, remove the previous year's leaves; in cooler areas, protect the crown with straw against cold; hates wet.

Musa basjoo (Japanese banana; basho): to 16 ft 3 in (5 m) tall; hardy to zone 8; a perennial with arching leaf blades; neutral to slightly acid, well-drained soil; the haiku poet Matsuo Basho (1644–94) took his name from this plant.

Foliage and Flowers

Foliage

Aspidistra elatior (ha-ran): hardy to zone 8; perennial with dark, glossy leaves; for tea gardens.

Farfugium japonicum (tsuwabuki): 1 ft (30 cm); hardy to zone 8; evergreen; partial or complete shade; glossy leaves; dislikes dry conditions.

Hosta spp. (plantain lilies; giboshi): partial or full shade, but yellow-leaved varieties appreciate some sun with midday protection; hates dry conditions; mulch in spring; leaves ovate, lance-shaped, round or heart-shaped; tall spikes of flowers in summer; *H. plantaginea* var. *japonica* (fragrant plantain lily; tama-no-kanzashi) has yellow-green leaves (hardy to zone 4); *H. sieboldiana* (seersucker plantain lily) has matte blue-green leaves (hardy to zone 4).

Rohdea japonica (omoto): hardy to zone 7; an evergreen perennial producing leathery leaves up to 1 ft (30 cm) in length; in summer produces greenish-yellow flower-heads followed by red or white berries; moist, acid soil in shade.

Flowers

Ajuga nipponensis (Japanese bugle; junihitoe): 4 to 9 in (10 to 25 cm) high; hardy to zone 8; perennial; pale pink flowers on short stems in spring.

Aster tartaricus (shion): to 6 ft 6 in (2 m); hardy to zone 3; a pale, delicate lavender aster flowering in autumn.

Astilbe (chidake-sashi): dwarf hybrids include "Sprite", which has dark foliage and pale pink flower-spikes in summer, growing to about 1 ft (30 cm) tall; hardy to zone 5; rich, moist soil in partial shade.

Begonia grandis subsp. *evansiana* (shukaido): to 1 ft 8 in (50 cm); hardy in zone 9, but protect against winter cold; perennial with fleshy stalks flushed red around the nodes; pale red single flowers from summer into autumn.

Bletilla striata (shi-ran): half-hardy to zone 7; a deciduous terrestrial orchid; moist, rich soil; partial shade; lance-shaped leaves; bright pink flowers in

spring to early summer; mulch in autumn, or lift and store in a dry, frost-free place.

Clintonia udensis (tsubame-omoto): 1 ft x 8 in (30 x 20 cm); hardy to zone 2; a herbaceous, clump-forming perennial; fertile, moist, neutral to acid soil; partial or full shade; bell-shaped white flowers in racemes in summer.

Disporum smilacinum (chigo-yuri): 8 to 10 in (20 to 25 cm) high; hardy to zone 6; perennial; one or two pendent flowers on each stem in spring; in groups as underplanting; partial shade.

Eupatorium fortunei (fujibakama): 3 ft 3 in (1 m); hardy in zone 9; moist soil; pale lavender umbels in autumn.

Filipendula purpurea (kyoganoko): 4 ft x 2 ft (1.2 m x 60 cm); hardy to zone 8; forms clumps of toothed leaves and feathery crimson flowers in summer; full sun to partial shade; good by water.

Gentiana makinoi (oyama-rindo): hardy to zone 6; herbaceous perennial; pale blue flowers in late summer; acid soil; plant between rocks.

Hemerocallis fulva (day lily; kanzo): hardy to zone 4; semi-evergreen perennial with trumpet-shaped orange flowers in late summer; sunny open ground, but does not like dry conditions.

Hepatica nobilis var. *japonica* (yuki-wari-so): hardy to zone 5; neutral, heavy soil in partial shade; a semi-evergreen perennial; star-shaped purple-blue flowers in early spring, often before leaves appear; resents being transplanted; also good for rock gardens.

Iris japonica (shaga): hardy to zone 4; flowers in spring to early summer; well-shaded, moist soil.

Liriope muscari (yabu-ran): hardy to zone 6; an evergreen perennial; produces pale lavender flower-spikes in autumn; acid soil; partial or complete shade; tolerant of drought; can be used as ground-cover.

Liriope spicata (ko-yabu-ran): 10 in x 1 ft 6 in (25 x 45 cm); hardy to zone 4; a semi-evergreen perennial; finely toothed leaves 8 in to 1 ft 4 in (20 to 40 cm) long; lavender to white flowers in late summer.

Physalis alkekengi (Chinese lantern; hozuki): hardy to zone 6; a hardy perennial; sun; grown for bright orange, papery, lantern-shaped seed pods in autumn.

Platycodon grandiflorum (balloon flower; kikyo): hardy in zones 6 and 7; purple (sometimes white or pink) flowers in early autumn, sometimes in summer; sunny, rich soil; flower-buds like tiny paper balloons before opening.

Polygonatum falcatum (fragrant Solomon's seal; naruko-yuri): hardy to zone 6; greenish-white delicate pendulous flowers along stem in late spring and early summer.

Tricyrtis hirta (toad lily; hototogisu): 2 to 3 ft 3 in (40 to 100 cm) high; hardy to zone 5; a clump-forming perennial; spotted purple flowers

in summer to early autumn; prefers moist, well-shaded conditions; plant in clumps.

Aquatic plants

Acorus gramineus (Japanese rush; sekisho): to 1 ft (30 cm); half-hardy to zone 6; a semi-evergreen perennial with narrow aromatic leaves for boggy ground, damp conditions, waterside; sun to partial shade; the dwarf variety needs very little soil so long as roots remain constantly wet.

Iris ensata (hana-shobu): hardy to zone 5; sun; keep roots moist from spring until autumn; keep dry during autumn and winter; split and repot after flowering; slightly acid aquatic soil; do not plant deep; the more fancy varieties are better suited for pot culture where the blooms can be admired close at hand; do not give too much nitrogenous fertilizer.

Iris laevigata (kakitsubata): hardy in zones 5 to 9; a marginal perennial; needs to have its roots wet all year round; good for a shelf in a pond.

Nelumbo nucifera (sacred lotus; hasu): tender; leaves up to 2 ft 8 in (80 cm) across; single or double, creamy-white or pink flowers in summer held on stalks well above leaves, up to 5 ft (1.5 m) above water level; sun; rich soil; from spring gradually increase water depth to 1 ft 4 in to 2 ft (40 to 60 cm) or 6 to 9 in (15 to 22 cm) for smaller cultivars; in frost zones, grow in containers, reduce water levels in autumn, overwinter in a frost-free place, ensuring that the rhizomes are kept moist.

Nymphaea spp. (water-lilies; suiren): deciduous, aquatic perennials; *N. tetragona* var. *tetragona*: a hardy (to zone 9) water-lily; small (1 to 2 in, 2.5 to 5 cm) white star-like blooms with yellow stamens; dwarf "Laydekerii" hybrids, in shades of red and pink, produced from this species.

facing page, from top left:
Skimmia japonica "Redruth", photographed in January
Liquidambar orientalis in November
Lilac (Syringa vulgaris)
Cornus stolonifera "Flaviramea", photographed in December

Non-traditional alternatives

Evergreens

Hebe cupressoides: 4 ft x 4 ft (1.2 x 1.2 m); hardy to zone 6; cypress-like leaves; flowers early to midsummer.

Myrtus communis (common myrtle): 14 ft 6 in x 9 ft 9 in (4.5 x 3 m); half-hardy in zones 6 to 8 with some shelter; dense and leafy; scented white flowers in late summer, purple-black fruits; *M. luma* is a little larger, with flaking cinnamon-colored bark; flowers in late summer.

Ozothamnus ledifolius: hardy to zone 7 with some shelter; a shrub from Tasmania with aromatic, dark green leaves, forming a round bush; *O. thyrosoides* (snow-in-summer) grows to 9 ft 9 in (3 m) and produces white flower-heads in summer.

Pachysandra terminalis (Japanese spurge; fukki-so): 10 in x 2 ft (25 x 60 cm); hardy to zone 4; evergreen ground-cover; prostrate glossy leaves in whorls; white berries; slightly acid to neutral soil, if the latter give plants acid fertilizer yearly; partial or deep shade; pinch out tips for the first two to three years.

Ruscus aculeatus (butcher's broom; nagi-ikada): 1 ft 8 in (50 cm); hardy to zone 6; male and female plants needed if red berries are wanted, unless a self-fertile variety is chosen; very shady conditions; use for underplanting and hedges.

Sarcococca confusa (sweet box): to 6 ft 6 in (2 m); a round shrub; fragrant, inconspicuous white flowers in winter; can be used as an informal hedge; shade; tolerates sun only if soil is moist.

Skimmia japonica (miyama-shikimi): 2 to 4 ft (60 cm to 1.2 m); hardy to zone 7; male and female plants needed if berries are wanted; poisonous red berries in the autumn, until spring.

Deciduous shrubs

Fothergilla gardenii (witch alder): to 3 ft 3 in (1 m); hardy to zone 4; a bushy shrub; fragrant flower-spikes like bottle-brushes in spring before leaves; good autumn leaf color; fertile, moist, acid soil in full sun.

Liquidambar orientalis (oriental sweet gum): to 19 ft 6 in (6 m); hardy to zone 8; a slow-growing, bushy tree; good autumn color, turning purple, orange and yellow; acid to neutral soil in sun; *L. styraciflua* "Moonbeam" grows even more slowly.

Flowering shrubs

Hibiscus syriacus (hibiscus; mukuge): 6 ft 6 in to 16 ft 3 in (2 to 5 m); hardy to zone 4; a deciduous shrub with erect branches; large flowers; sun but will tolerate shade; fast-growing; used for hedging; very popular in Japan for informal gardens; *H. mutabilis* (Confederate rose mallow, fuyo) has mallow-like flowers.

Leycesteria formosa (Himalayan honeysuckle): 6 ft 6 in x 6 ft 6 in (2 x 2 m); hardy to zone 7; forms thickets; attractive white flowers with brownish-purple bracts in summer to early autumn; sun or partial shade; in colder areas mulch deeply before winter.

Syringa vulgaris (common lilac): hardy to zone 4; prune back in winter when first planted to encourage bushy growth; many varieties available.

Winter interest

Alnus incana (grey alder); *Alnus glutinosa* (common alder): hardy to zone 2; many garden varieties for wet but well-drained situations (*A. incana* will tolerate drier soils); pendulous catkins and brown cone-like fruit on bare branches in late winter; handsome foliage.

Cornus alba (red-barked dogwood): 9 ft 9 in x 9 ft 9 in (3 x 3 m); hardy to zone 3; red stems in winter; prune to the ground in spring for new growth; good autumn leaf color; good waterside shrub.

Cornus stolonifera (red osier dogwood): hardy to zone 2; "Midwinter Fire" produces red and yellow stems; "Winter Beauty" has striking orange branches.

Salix alba var. *vitellina* (golden willow): bright yellow to orange winter shoots; "Britzensis" has orange-red winter shoots and "Chermesina" has bright red shoots.

Salix caprea "Kilmarnock" (Kilmarnock willow): 5 ft to 6 ft 6 in (1.5 to 2 m); hardy to zone 5; a weeping willow with grey catkins in the early spring; suitable for smaller gardens.

Viburnum grandiflorum: 8 ft x 8 ft (2.5 x 2.5 m); hardy to zone 6; a deciduous shrub; fragrant pink-flushed flower clusters on leafless branches during winter.

"Wild" flowers

Astrantia major (masterwort): 1 to 3 ft x 1 ft 6 in (30 to 90 cm x 45 cm); hardy to zone 7; a clump-forming, hardy perennial; small, pale pink, five-petalled flowers, surrounded by white bracts, early to midsummer, sometimes later; moist, rich soil, tolerates some dryness; sun or partial shade; *A. maxima* is a little taller.

Kirengeshoma palmata (ki-renge-shoma): 2 to 4 ft (60 to 120 cm); hardy to zone 5; clumps of broad leaves and slender stalks with pale yellow tubular flowers; moist, acid soil in partial shade; mulch with leaf-mould.

Meconopsis cambrica (Welsh poppy): hardy to zone 6; flowers in yellow, orange or even red; grows in dry places like the base of hedges, and seeds itself very easily.

Trillium grandiflorum: the great white trillium of North America; *T. kamtschaticum* (enrei-so): an indigenous Japanese species to about 8 in (20 cm)

in height; three-petalled reddish-purple flowers in spring; moist, rich, deep, acid to neutral soil in shade; both species are hardy to zone 5.

Foliage plants

Chamaemelum nobilis "Treneague" (chamomile): hardy to zone 4; non-flowering variety; suitable ground-cover.

Festuca glauca: hardy to zone 6; an evergreen perennial grass forming dense tufts of spiky bluish-grey leaves to 8 in (20 cm) long.

Helictotrichon sempervirens (blue oat grass): hardy to zone 6; a tufted grass, evergreen and perennial, with grey-blue leaves up to 10 in (25 cm) long; well-drained alkaline soil; sun.

Heuchera cylindrica (coral flower); 1 ft to 1 ft 8 in x 1 ft (30 to 50 cm x 30 cm); hardy to zone 4; a perennial for moist, rich, well-drained neutral soil; sun or partial or complete shade; round-lobed dark green leaves; creamy-colored flowers in spring to midsummer on ends of long stems; also *H. micrantha* and several cultivars, esp. "Pewter Moon".

Phormium tenax (New Zealand flax): hardy to zone 7 with some shelter; a clump-forming, evergreen perennial with rigid, architectural leaves to 9 ft 9 in (3 m); many variegated cultivars.

Phuopsis stylosa: hardy to zone 6; good ground-cover for dry soils; spreads slowly; pink pincushion flower-heads; *P.s.* "Purpurea" has purple flowers.

Thymus serpyllum (creeping thyme): hardy to zone 5; excellent ground-cover; well-drained, poor soil in full sun or partial shade; if it begins to get straggly, prune hard before flowering.

Yucca gloriosa (Spanish dagger): 4 ft (1.5 m); hardy to zone 9 with some shelter; an architectural plant for large gardens; needs sun and well-drained soil, especially in winter; sharp, stiff leaves and spikes of bell-shaped white flowers in late summer to autumn.

Aquatic plants

Iris pseudacorus (yellow flag): 3 to 5 ft (90 cm to 1.5 m); hardy to zone 7; yellow flowers in mid to late summer; vigorous.

Iris versicolor (blue flag): 1 ft 2 in to 2 ft (35 to 60 cm); hardy to zone 7; flowers early to midsummer. *I. virginica* (southern blue flag) is slightly less hardy.

Lysichiton camtschatcensis (bog arum; mizu-basho): spreading to 2 ft 6 in (75 cm); hardy to zone 6; marginal aquatic perennials, white spathes produced early in spring.

facing page, from top left:

Welsh poppy (Meconopsis cambrica)
Yellow flag iris (Iris pseudacorus)
Yucca gloriosa
Trillium grandiflorum

Hardiness
Zones

Great Britain and
western Europe

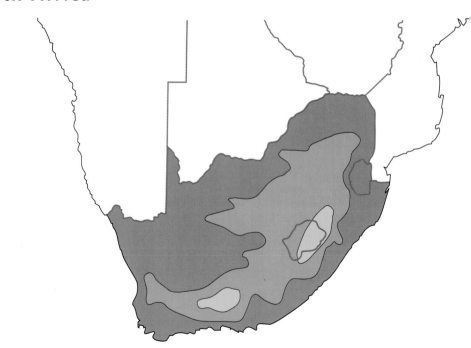

South Africa

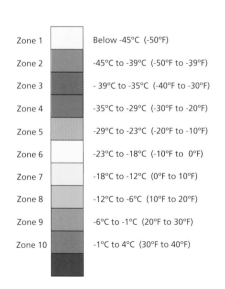

Zone 1		Below -45°C (-50°F)
Zone 2		-45°C to -39°C (-50°F to -39°F)
Zone 3		- 39°C to -35°C (-40°F to -30°F)
Zone 4		-35°C to -29°C (-30°F to -20°F)
Zone 5		-29°C to -23°C (-20°F to -10°F)
Zone 6		-23°C to -18°C (-10°F to 0°F)
Zone 7		-18°C to -12°C (0°F to 10°F)
Zone 8		-12°C to -6°C (10°F to 20°F)
Zone 9		-6°C to -1°C (20°F to 30°F)
Zone 10		-1°C to 4°C (30°F to 40°F)

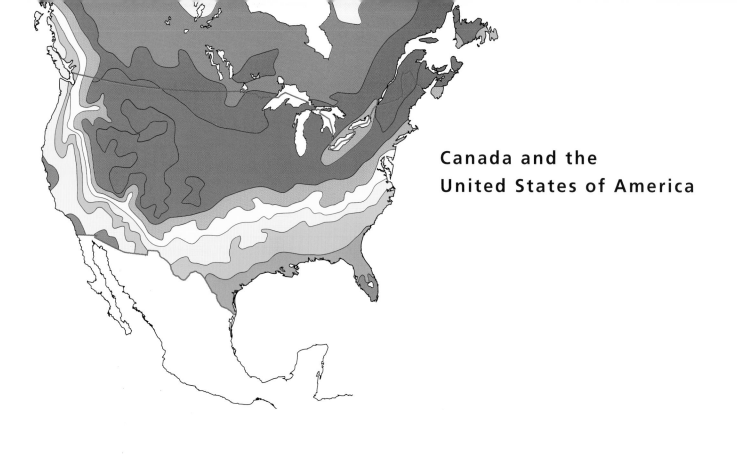

**Canada and the
United States of America**

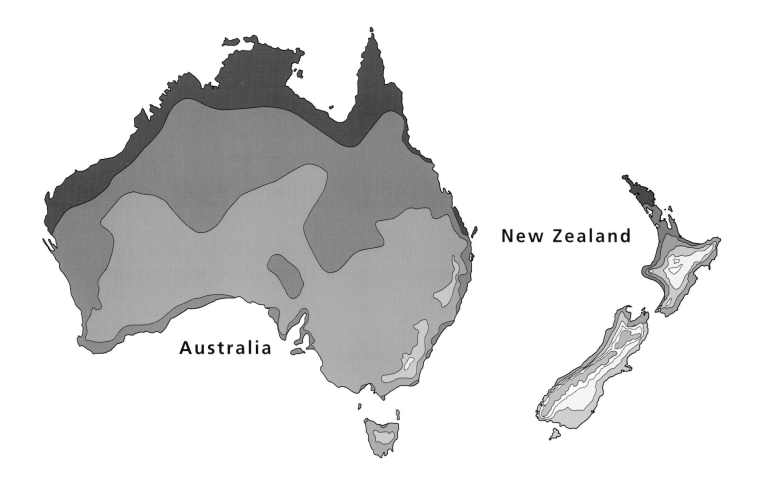

New Zealand

Australia

Bibliography

Aoki, Koichiro. *Edo no engei* [Gardening in Edo]. Tokyo: Chikuma Shobo, 1998.

Bessatsu Taiyo. *Kyo no koniwa* [Small Gardens of Kyoto] 78 (Summer 1992).

Cave, Philip. *Creating Japanese Gardens*. London: Aurum Press, 1993.

Conder, Josiah. *Landscape Gardening in Japan*. Yokohama: Kelly & Walsh, 1893.

Davidson, A. K. *The Art of Zen Gardens: A Guide to their Creation and Enjoyment*. Los Angeles: Jeremy P. Tarcher, 1983.

Du Cane, Florence. *The Flowers and Gardens of Japan*. London: Adam and Charles Black, 1908.

Engel, David H. *A Thousand Mountains, A Million Hills: Creating the Rock Work of Japanese Gardens*. Tokyo: Shufu-no-tomo-sha/Japan Publications, 1995.

Funakoshi, Ryoji. *Hanaki niwaki no seishi sentei* [Maintaining and Pruning Flowering and Garden Trees]. Tokyo: Shufu-no-tomo-sha, 1990.

Glattstein, Judy. *Enhance Your Garden with Japanese Plants: A Practical Source Book*. New York: Kodansha, 1996.

Japanese Garden Society of Oregon, with Kate Jerome. *Oriental Gardening*. New York: Pantheon Books, 1996.

Kanto, Shigemori. *The Japanese Courtyard Garden: Landscapes for Small Spaces*. Trans. Pamela Pasti. New York and Tokyo: Weatherhill, 1981. (Originally published as *Kyoto tsubo niwa* [Courtyard Gardens of Kyoto]. Kyoto: Mitsumura-suiko-shoin, 1980.)

Katagiri, Keiko. *Juki* [Trees]. Photography by Yoichiro Kaneda. Tokyo: Seito-sha, 1996.

Keane, Marc P. *Japanese Garden Design*. Rutland, Vermont and Tokyo: Charles E. Tuttle, 1996.

Kunishige, Masaaki and Funakoshi, Ryoji (eds). *Niwaki Hanaki* [Garden and Flowering Trees]. Tokyo: Nippon Hoso Shuppan Kyokai, 1991.

Mitford, Algernon Bertram Freeman-, 1st Baron Redesdale. *The Bamboo Garden*. London: Macmillan, 1896.

Mitsuhashi, Kazuo and Takahashi, Ichiro. *Wagaya no niwazukuri* [Creating Gardens at Home]. Tokyo: Shufu-to-seikatsu-sha, 1984.

Miyamoto, Kenji. *Nihonteien no Mikata* [Looking at Japanese Gardens]. Kyoto: Gakugei Shuppan, 1998.

Mizuno, Katsuhiko. *Kyoto hana no meitei sanpo* [A Stroll Through the Famous Flower Gardens of Kyoto]. Tokyo: Kodansha, 1997.

Nippon Zoen Kumiai Rengo (ed.). *Niwaki no sentei: kotsu to tabu* [Pruning Garden Trees: Practical Hints and Taboos]. Tokyo: Kodansha, 1996.

Nitschke, Günter. *Japanese Gardens: Right Angle and Natural Form*. Berlin: Benedikt Taschen, 1993.

Ohashi, Haruzo (photographer). *Chatei: The Tea Garden*. Tokyo: Graphic-sha, 1989.

Ohashi, Haruzo (photographer). *The Indoor Garden*. Tokyo: Graphic-sha, 1987.

Ono, Masaaki (ed.). *Tsuboniwa no susume* [Creating Courtyard Gardens]. Tokyo: Kodansha, 1994.

Oster, Maggie. *Japanese Garden Style: Eastern Traditions in Western Garden Design*. London: Cassell, 1993.

Saito, Katsuo and Wada, Sadaji. *Magic of Trees and Stones: Secrets of Japanese Gardening*. New York: Japan Publications, 1964.

Seike, Kiyoshi and Kudo, Masanobu. *A Japanese Touch for your Garden*. Tokyo: Kodansha, 1995.

Shirahata, Yozaburo. *Daimyoteien* [Daimyo Gardens]. Tokyo: Kodansha, 1997.

Tanaka, Seidai. *Nippon no teien* [Gardens of Japan]. Tokyo: Kashima Shuppankai, 1967.

Tatsui Teien Kenkyusho (ed.). *Karesansui no hanashi* [About Dry Gardens]. Tokyo: Kenchiku-shiryo-kenkyusha, 1991.

Tatsui Teien Kenkyusho (ed.). *Suikinkutsu no hanashi* [About Musical Water Features]. Tokyo: Kenchiku-shiryo-kenkyusha, 1990.

Tatsui Teien Kenkyusho (ed.). *Takegaki no hanashi* [About Bamboo Fences]. Tokyo: Kenchiku-shiryo-kenkyusha, 1990.

Yoshikawa, Isao. *Japanese Stone Gardens: Appreciation and Creation*. Tokyo: Graphic-sha, 1992.

Yoshikawa, Isao. *Puro ni manabu takegakizukuri* [Learning How to Make Bamboo Fences the Professional Way]. Tokyo: Graphic-sha, 1997.

Yoshikawa, Isao. *Takegaki no dezain* [Bamboo Fence Designs]. Tokyo: Graphic-sha, 1988.

Gardens to visit

Asticou Azalea Garden, Seal Harbor And Peabody Drive, Northeast Harbor, Mount Desert Island, Maine

Bloedel Reserve, 7571 N.E. Dolphin Drive, Bainbridge Island, Washington
Tel: (206) 842-7631 (by reservation only)

Golden Gate Park, Fell and Stanyan Streets, San Francisco, California
Tel: (415) 831-2700

Huntington Library Botanical Gardens, 1151 Oxford Road, San Marino, California
Tel: (818) 405-2141

Japanese Friendship Garden, 2125 Park Blvd, San Diego, California
Tel: (619) 232-2721

Japanese Garden, Washington Park, 611 S.W. Kingston Ave., Portland, Oregon
Tel: (503) 223-4070

Japanese Garden at the Museum of Fine Arts, 465 Huntington Ave, Boston
Tel: (617) 267-9300

Japanese Hill and Pond Garden, Brooklyn Botanic Garden, 1000 Washington Ave., Brooklyn, New York
Tel: (718) 622-4433

Kubota Gardens, 9600 Renton Avenue South, Seattle

Kumamoto-en, San Antonio Botanical Gardens, 555 Funston Place, San Antonio, Texas
Tel: (210) 207-3250

Ordway Japanese Garden, Como Park Conservatory, 1325 Aida Place, St. Paul, Minnesota
Tel: (612) 487-8240

Sansho-en, Chicago Botanic Garden, 1000 Lake Cook Road, Glencoe, Illinois
Tel: (847) 835-5440

Seiwa-en, Missouri Botanical Garden, 4344 Shaw Blvd., St Louis, Missouri
Tel: (314) 577-5100

Washington Park Arboretum and Japanese Garden, University of Washington, 2300 Arboretum Drive East, Seattle, Washington
Tel: (206) 543-8800

CANADA:

Kurimoto Japanese Garden, Devonian Botanic Garden (University of Alberta), Route 60, Edmonton, Alberta
Tel: (403) 987-3054

Nitobe Memorial Garden, University of British Columbia Botanical Garden, 6804 S.W. Marine Drive, Vancouver, British Columbia
Tel: (604) 822-9666

Photography credits & acknowledgements

Garden Picture Library: David Askham 106-107; Mark Bolton 125tr; Philippe Bonduel 131tr; Brian Carter 137tl; Christi Carter 127tr, 129tl; Eric Crichton 137tr; John Glover 131bl, 131br, 135tl; Sunniva Harte 137br; Neil Holmes 127tl; Lamontagne 107r, 125tl, 129br; John Neubauer 125bl; Joanne Pavia 40; Howard Rice 127bl, 135tr, 135br; Gary Rogers 104; JS Sira 133tl; Ron Sutherland 16, 56, 120-121, 122-123; Juliette Wade 135bl; Rachel White 3. **Jerry Harpur:** 11, 13, 18-19, 21, 25, 26, 29, 32, 35, 36, 37, 47, 55, 62-63, 69tr, 66bl, 70, 71, 73t, 73b, 76, 79, 82-83, 85, 93, 96, 100, 103, 108, 109, 110, 114; des. MP Keane 57, 58-59; des. Jeff Mendoza 38; Mrs Pomeroy, CA 44, 61, 66, 69tl, 92; Terry Welch 9, 95. **Sunniva Harte:** 1, 20, 28, 34, 45, 52, 84, 86, 87. **Anne Hyde:** 14. **JTB Photo Library:** 24. **Marc Peter Keane:** 46a. **Andrew Lawson:** 22, 64-65, 67, 74, 98, 105, 111. **Marianne Majerus:** des. Peter Chan and Brenda Sacoor 27, 39, 81. **Kazuo Mitsuhashi:** 77, 99, 102. **Clive Nichols:** 6-7, 12, 15, 75, 129tr; des. Richard Coward 90; des. Dowle & K Ninomiya 4, 88; des. Robert Ketchell & Eileen Tunnell 119. **Katsutoshi Okada:** 30-31, 48-49, 51, 54. **Photos Horticultural:** 125br, 127br, 129bl, 131tl, 133tr, 133bl, 133br, 137bl. **David Scott:** 41, 69br. **Tony Stone Images:** David Ball 8. **Patrick Taylor:** 113. **Pamla Toler:** des. Paul Sheppard 59r, 60 (des. Paul Sheppard, K. Wood). **Elizabeth Whiting & Associates:** 42, 50, 94. **Isao Yoshikawa:** 115, 116, 117.

I am very grateful to Yvonne McFarlane at New Holland Publishers for the opportunity to write on a subject which has been very important to me since I first heard of the courtyard garden which my great-grandfather created. I wish also to thank Anke Ueberberg and Christine Rista at New Holland for their help in putting this book together. It has been a pleasure to work with Grahame Dudley, the designer, and Sandra Pond, the illustrator. This book could not have taken shape without the close editing of Sandra Raphael. Her advice and support have guided me through a daunting task.

I wish to thank the photographers who have permitted their work to be used in this book, and the owners and designers of the remarkable gardens which it is a privilege to present to readers. Mike and Alice Sharland gave me the confidence to embark on this project. Abbot Shodo Maeda of Zuiho-in, Daitoku-ji Temple, Kyoto, and Mr and Mrs Toshifumi Saimon have generously shared with me their deep store of knowledge about gardens and Japanese architecture. I owe a profound debt of gratitude to my parents, not least for their efforts in helping to locate elusive reference material. Without their support, I could not have written this book. Finally, I wish to thank my husband for his enthusiasm, his patience and his faith in me.

First published in the United States of America in 2000 by Trafalgar Square Publishing, North Pomfret, Vermont 05053

Printed and bound in Singapore by Tien Wah Press (Pte) Ltd

Copyright © 2000 in text Yoko Kawaguchi
Copyright © 2000 in photography
see picture credits
Copyright © 2000 New Holland Publishers (UK) Ltd

ISBN 1-57076-164-7

Library of Congress
Catalog Card Number: 00-100130

Designer: Grahame Dudley
Editor: Sandra Raphael
Project Editor and
 Picture Researcher: Christine Rista
Assistant Editor: Anke Ueberberg
Production: Caroline Hansell

Editorial Direction: Yvonne McFarlane

4 6 8 10 9 7 5 3

Reproduction by Modern Age Repro House Ltd, Hong Kong

General index

Page numbers in *italics* denote illustrations

Please note: Japanese surnames precede first names.

acidity of soil 17, 74
aquatic plants 84, 90, 134, 136
Ashikaga, Yoshimasa 44
asymmetry 72–3
Augsburg, *oki-gata* lantern *111*

basins: *see* water basins
Batsford Park *12*
berries 130
Bloedel Reserve *96*
bonsai trees 13, 14
borrowed vistas 120
Bridge to Heaven 23, 86
bridges: humpback 104, *107*; lakes 23; ornamental *26*; raft-like *108*; rock 87; stepping-stones *104*; stone slabs *120–1*; turf 104, *108*; wooden *104*; *yatsuhashi 84, 104, 105, 106, 108, 109*
Brown, Lancelot "Capability" 8
Buddhist temples, paradise gardens 23
Buddhist tradition, rock groupings 81, 83; *see also* Zen Buddhist influences

calligraphy 37
carp rocks 29, 87
cascades *14*, 87, 91, *92*
Chambers, Sir William 8
Chan, Peter *27*, *81*
Chelsea Flower Show, Honda Tea Garden *88*
Chinese gardens 8
Chinese Pagoda, Kew Gardens 8
Chinese scroll paintings 35, 37
Chion-in Temple, rock groupings 83
Christianity, temple garden 37
color effects 26
concealment, partial 29, 32, 51, 57, 93
Conder, Josiah 13
Coombe Wood, Surrey 14
Cottered, Hertfordshire 14
courtyard gardens 48, *58–9*; fencing 61; gravel *54–5*; plants 61, 63; rocks *57*, *62*
Coward, Richard *90*
crane rocks 37, *77*, 83
cypress logs, pergolas 112

Daisen-in, rock garden 35
decking 32, 33, 55, 93
distance creating 29, 32, 81
Dowle, J. *88*
dry gardens 34–5, *36*, 37, 40–3; designing 40; gravel *38*, 40; moss 43; plants 40, 43, 63; rocks 35, 37; sand 37; Seattle *9*

erosion prevention 33
evergreens 89, 119

Fairchild, David 13
fencing: bamboo 29, 114, 117, *118*; brushwood/reed 117, *118*, 119; courtyard garden 61; *ginkakuji* 117; *hagi* 117; *kenninji* 114, *116*, 117, *118*; *kinkakuji* 114; *koetsuji* 119; *kuromoji* 117; rustic-style *115*; *ryoanji* 114; *shimizu* 117; sleeve *50*, *54*, 55, 57, 117; *takeho* 117; *teppo 54*, *118*; wooden *45*; *yarai 7*, 40, *41*, *71*, 114, 119; *yotsume* 29, *118*
fish 90
flower petals 53
flowers 134
foliage 134, 136
Fortune, Robert 13
Freeman-Mitford, A. B. 13
Fudaraku, Mount 80
Furuta, Oribe 49–50, 52

gate, *torii* 8, 27, 29
gateway 29
The Geisha 10
Gilbert, W. S. 10
granite slabs *46*
gravel: beaches *27*; courtyard garden *54–5*; dry gardens *38*, 40; as stream 87
Greville, Louis 13
ground-cover 130; courtyard garden 63; dry gardens 43; hills 25; tea garden 51; waterfalls 87, 89

Hampton Court Flower Show 119, *129*
hardiness zones 138–9
Heale House, Wiltshire 13, 14
hedges 43, 53, 73
hill and pond gardens *15*, 20–1, 23–5, *30–1*, *41*; designing 26–7, 29, 32
hill and pond stroll gardens *85*
hills, man-made 24–5
Honda Tea Garden *88*
Horai, Mount 80, 81, 83
Hornel, E. A. 14

Ichi-riki-tei garden *48*, *54*
Iford Manor 14
islands 20, 23
Iwasa family *30*

Japan 8, 10
Japanese Garden, Portland *34*, *84*
Japanese gardens 8, 10, 13, 17
Jizo-in Temple 83

Kasuga Shrine 110
Katsura Palace gardens 23–4, 111
Keane, Marc Peter *46*, *57*, *59*
Kenrokuen Park *110*
Ketchell, Robert *119*
Kew Gardens, Chinese Pagoda 8
kimono 98
Kobori, Enshu 49, 50, 51, 52, 101
Konchi-in, Nanzen-ji Temple 101
Kyoto: court life 20; courtyard gardens 48; hill and pond garden *30–1*; moss gardens 43; sand 96

lakes 20, 23
landscape: diversity 14–15, 26; local 17; natural 7, 8; recreated 19, 20–1, 65
lanterns 110; *ikegomi-gata 110*; *kasuga 6–7*, 8, 44, 45, 57, 110; *kotoji 110*; with legs *110*; *oki-gata 43*, 110, *111*; *oribe 50*, *56*, pagoda style *111*; square/no shaft *42*, *43*; *tachi-gata 110*; toadstool-shaped *26*; water areas 85, 111; water basins 94; *yukimi-gata 61*, *86*, *111*
leaves, fallen 53, *103*
Lenz Garden *122-23*
Liberty, Arthur Lasenby 10
Loti, Pierre 10

Madame Butterfly 10
man-made and natural materials 79
Matsuo, Basho 1, 134
Max Koch Garden *16*, *120–1*
Maximowicz, Carl Johann 13
medicinal plants 17
Mendoza, Jeff *38*
Messager, André 10
The Mikado 10
millstones *46*, 101
Monet, Claude 14
moss gardens 43
Mount Ephraim, Kent 14
Murasaki Shikibu (Lady) 20
mythology 23, 37, 80

naturalists 10, 13
nature 7, 17, 19, 27, 120
Ninomiya, K. *88*
NJ Landscapes *106*

open spaces 24

paradise gardens 23
passageway gardens 44
paths 98–9, 101, 103

Paul, Anthony *120-21*, 124
pebbles 51, 59, 86, 90, 91
pergolas 59, 89, 112
perimeter planting 33
Peto, Harold 14
pine needles 53
Plantbessin *112*, *113*
plant collectors 13
ponds 29, 84, 86–7, *89*; concrete 89–90; fish 90; glass roof *60*; pine stake borders 87; shapes 84, *89*
privacy 52, 61
privy, ornamental 49
pruning 20, 51, 65, 66, 69, 113
Puccini, Giacomo 10
pumps for streams 93
purification 49

Sen-no-Rikyu 44, 47, 49, 52, 53, 110
Ritsurin Park *41*, 69
rock garden 35, 63
rocks 23, 29, 76; arrangements 78; boat-shaped 81; Buddha stone group 81; as carp 87; cascades 87, 91, *92*; conifers *81*; courtyard garden *56*, *62*; as crane 37, *77*, 83; cut 105; dry gardens 35, 37; embedded 27, 76, 78, 83; granite slabs *46*; grouping 65, 76, 78, 80–1, 83, *96*; for meditation 81; shape/quality 37, 76–7, 80; standing 8, *9*, *22*; stroll garden 80; as turtle 37, 40, *77*, 83; water basins 94, 110; as waterfall 57, 89
roji 50, 53, *102*; *see also* tea garden
Ryoan-ji Temple 35, 37, *71*, *73*, 94
Ryugen-in Temple *100*

sabi 44
Sacoor, Brenda 27, *81*
sacred spaces 27, 29
safety, water features 93
Sainte-Beuve, Collette and Hubert *112*, *113*
Saint-Saëns, Camille 10
sand 89, 96, 97; patterns *97*
sand spit 23, 86, 111
sanzonseki 81
scalene triangle groupings 73, *77*, 78, *96*
screening 51, 57, *119*
seasonal changes 15, 123
Seattle dry garden *9*
shapes: basins 94; plants 66–7, 70; ponds 84, 89; rocks 76, 77, 80
Sheppard, Paul *59*
shrines 29
shrubs 66, *82*, 128, 130, 134, 136; *see also plants index*
Shugakuin Palace garden 23, *74*

Shumisen mountain 81
Siebold, Philipp Franz von 10, 13
Silverstream, dry garden *39*
spirituality 27, 96
standing stones 8, *9*, *22*
stepping-stones 47, 51, 87, 98–9, *100*, 101, *104*
stones: *see* rocks
stream beds, laying *91*
streams 90–1, 89, *92*
stroll garden 23, 24, *75*, 80, *85*
Sullivan, Arthur 10
Sung period scroll paintings 35, 37

Tabuchi family *102*
The Tale of Genji (Shikibu) 20
Tatton Park *6-7*, 14, *75*
tea ceremony 44, 52
tea garden 23–4; changing tableaux 50–1; inner/outer gardens 44–5, 47; intimacy 49; light 52; planting 51, 53; stepping-stones 98; water basins 94
teahouse entrance *46*
temple gardens 34–5, 37
Thunberg, Carl Pehr 10, 13
timelessness 7, 17, 23
topiary *68*, 70, 72
Toyotomi, Hideyoshi 44, 52
tranquillity 7, 17, 27, 44
trees 66, 124, 126, 128; *see also plants index*
tsukubai 94, 110
tufa 76, *77–8*
Tully, near Kildare 14
Tunnell, Eileen *119*
turtle rocks 37, 40, 83

underplanting 33, 53, 63

vantage point 24, 37, 55, 93
Veitch, James 14
Veitch, James Gould 13, 14

wabi 44
walls, whitewashed 119, 120
water, Chinese pictogram 84
water basins 57, *94*; bamboo scoop *95*; plants 52, 53; streams *91*; tea garden 47, 49, *50*
waterfalls 87, 89
Watson, Fred *109*
Welch, Terry *79*
Westonbirt Arboretum *125*
Wilson, E. H. 13, 14

Zen Buddhist influences 14, 34–5, 37
Zen gardens *77*, 81, *82*
Zuiho-in temple garden 37

Index of plants

Acer japonicum 125, 126; *A. palmatum* 13, 40, 126; *A. p.* var. *heptalobum* 13, 126; *A. p.* var. *matsumurae* 126; *A. rubrum* 13
Acorus calamus 84; *A. gramineus* 10, 33, 84, 134
Adiantum aleuticum 132
Ajuga nipponensis 33, 63, 134
Akebia quinata 59
Albizia julibrissin 33
alders 26, 136
Alisma plantago-aquatica 120
Alnus incana 136; *A. glutinosa* 136
andromeda 33, 73, 128
anemone 43, 78
apricot 33, 40, 43, 51, 94, 123, 128
Aquilegia 63
Ardisia crispa 43, 63, 74, 98, 123, 127, 130; *A. japonica* 29, 33, 63, 128
Arenaria tetraquetra 132
aspidistra 59
Aspidistra elatior 43, 53, 134
Aster tartaricus 43, 123, 134
astilbe 32, 43, 84, 134
Astilboides tabularis 84
Astrantia major 136; *A. maxima* 136
Athyrium nipponicum 132
Aucuba japonica 10, 29, 53, 54, 57, 128
azalea 10, 73; acid soils 74; by bridges 20; deciduous 66, 123; embankments 33; hedging 43; round pruned 29, 30, 34, 35, 40, 70, 73

balloon plant 43, 53, 123, 134; dry rock garden 63; hill planting 21; in moss 108; underplanting 33;
bamboo 53, 61, 130, 132; dry gardens 35; Freeman-Mitford 113; lower branches removed 57, 68; transplanting 63;
bamboo grass 29, 33, 40, 70, 132
Bambusa multiplex 132
banana (Japanese) 63, 134
barberry 128
beauty-berry 33, 130
Begonia grandis subsp. *evansiana* 32, 98, 131, 134
Berberis thunbergii 128
black pine 72, 124
Blechnum nipponicum 132
Bletilla striata 63, 134
bog arum 136
box 124, 136
blue flag 84, 136
bugle 33, 63, 134
bush clover 20, 21, 43, 117, 130
butcher's broom 136
buttercup witch hazel 33, 128
Buxus microphylla var. *japonica* 124

Calanthe discolor 63
Callicarpa dichotoma 91, 130; *C. japonica* 33, 130
camellia 126; acid soils 74; dry gardens 40; 18th century 15; grouping 73; trimmed 67
Camellia japonica 43, 126; *C. sasanqua* 43, 66, 126
Carex hachijoensis 132
carpet grass 86
Carpinus betulus 26
Castanopsis cuspidata 43, 53, 124
cedar 33, 124
Cercidiphyllum japonicum 126
Cercis chinensis 26, 126
Chamaecyparis obtusa 33, 72; *C. pisifera* 124
Chamaemelum nobilis 136
chamomile 40, 136
cherry: flowering 13, 33, 40, 43, 66; weeping 33; Yoshino 70

Chimonobambusa spp. 63; *C. marmorea* 132; *C. quadrangularis* 43, 132
Chinese hawthorn 128
Chinese holly 29, 67, 70, 124
Chinese lantern 43, 63, 131, 134
Chinese redbud 26, 126
Chinese silvergrass 43, 132
chrysanthemum 15
Citrus tachibana 15, 43, 73, 98
Clerodendrum trichotomum 126
Cleyera japonica 43, 51, 53, 70, 73, 124
Clintonia udensis 134
columbines 63
Commelina communis 63
conifers 20, 69
Conocephalum conicum 132
coral flower 136
Cornus alba 136; *C. kousa* 26, 43, 74, 123, 126; *C. officinalis* 123, 126; *C. stolonifera* 135, 136
Corylopsis pauciflora 33, 73, 128
crabapple 17, 33
crape myrtle 10, 43, 74, 125, 126
Cryptomeria japonica 33, 33, 68, 124
Cycas revoluta 43, 63, 129, 134
Cymbidium goeringii 33
cypress, hinoki 72, 120
Cypripedium japonicum 33
Cyrtomium macrophyllum 132

daimio oak 43
daphne 57, 74
Daphne odora 57, 67, 128
Daphniphyllum macropodum 53, 66, 73, 124
Davallia mariesii 132
day lily 43, 133, 134
Dendropanax trifidus 53, 66, 124
Deutzia gracilis 128
Diospyros kaki 33
Disporum smilacinum 53, 134
dogwood 136
Dryopteris erythrosora 132

enkianthus 20, 52, 68, 74
Enkianthus campanulatus 128; *E. cernuus* f. *rubens* 130; *E. perulatus* 53, 130
Equisetum hiemale 33, 51, 53, 57, 63, 132
Erythronium japonicum 33
euonymus, winged 110, 127, 128
Euonymus alatus 33, 43, 110, 127, 128; *E. hamiltonianus* subsp. *sieboldianus* 126; *E. japonicus* 72, 124, 125
Eupatorium fortunei 134; *E. japonicum* 63
Eurya emarginata 43, 128; *E. japonica* 33, 43, 53, 128

Farfugium japonicum 33, 43, 53, 103, 131, 134
Fargesia murieliae 129
Fatsia japonica 32, 54, 63, 125, 128
ferns 29, 32, 36, 51, 53, 59, 63, 132
Festuca glauca 136
filipendula 84
Filipendula purpurea 32, 134
flax, New Zealand 136
Forsythia suspensa 43
Fothergilla gardenii 136

gentian 63
Gentiana makinoi 134
Ginkgo biloba 53, 126
grasses 43, 86, 99, 132, 136

Hakonechloa macra 132
Hamamelis japonica 126
Hebe cupressoides 136
heavenly bamboo 53, 61, 130
Helictotrichon sempervirens 136
Hemerocallis spp. 43; *H. fulva* 43, 133, 134
hemlock 33
Hepatica spp. 63, 134
Heuchera cylindrica 136
hiba arborvitae 70, 124
Hibanobambusa tranquillans 132
Hibiscus syriacus 136; *H. mutabilis* 136

hinoki cypress 72, 120
holly: box-leaved 24, 30, 33, 40, 53, 67, 70, 73, 110, 124; Chinese 29, 67, 70, 124
hornbeam 26
horsetail 33, 51, 53, 57, 63
Hosta spp. 21, 33, 53, 134; *H. plantaginea* 10
Hydrangea spp. 33, 52; *H. macrophylla* 52, 127, 130; *H. paniculata* 53, 130

Ilex crenata 24, 30, 33, 53, 67, 70, 73, 110, 124; *I. integra* 33, 53, 53, 67, 70, 110, 124; *I. rotunda* 124; *I. serrata* 33, 43, 110, 128
Imperata cylindrica "Rubra" 132
iris 99, 120; *see also* blue flag; yellow flag
Iris ensata 24, 33, 84, 124, 133, 134; *I. japonica* 33, 43, 43, 63, 134; *I. laevigata* 17, 33, 84, 90, 108, 120, 134; *I. pseudacorus* 84, 136, 137; *I. versicolor* 84, 136

Juniperus chinensis 20, 33, 66, 69, 124; *J. c.* var. *procumbens* 43, 128

kerria 10
Kerria japonica 130
Kirengeshoma palmata 136
kuromoji 114

lady's slipper 33
Lagerstroemia indica 10, 43, 125, 126
laurel 33, 53, 54, 57, 128
Lespedeza spp. 20, 33, 43, 117, 130
Leycesteria formosa 136
Ligustrum japonicum 43, 70
lilac 135, 136
lily: arum 87; bog arum 136; day 43, 133, 134; plantain 10, 134; toad 33, 43, 53, 63, 123, 134; trout 33
Lindera umbellata 117
Liquidambar orientalis 135, 136; *L. styraciflua* 136
liriope 29, 47, 51
Liriope muscari 43, 51, 55, 63, 131, 134; *L. spicata* 134
Lithocarpus edulis 43, 124
lotus flower 23, 84, 133, 134
Lysichiton camtschatcensis 136

Magnolia grandiflora 33; *M. hypoleuca* 126; *M. kobus* 126; *M. liliiflora* 126; *M. salicifolia* 126; *M. sieboldii* 126; *M. stellata* 126; *M. wieseneri* 128
Mahonia japonica 17, 128
maidenhair tree 53, 126
Malus floribunda 33
mandarin orange 15, 43, 98
maple 91, 125, 126; acid soils 74; bonsai 13; by bridges 26, 33; dry gardens 35, 40; groupings 73; leaf color 15, 40, 55, 66, 75; by pond 29; shapes 57, 59; by waterfall 89; *see also* Acer
Marchantia polymorpha 132
marlberry 29, 128
masterwort 136
Matteuccia struthiopteris 63, 132
Meconopsis cambrica 136, 137
Miscanthus sinensis 43, 43, 123, 129, 132
mondo grass 130
morning glory 15
moss 43, 132; courtyard gardens 54, 59; dry gardens 40; ground cover 29, 47; islands 76; stepping-stones 51, 53; by stream 91
Musa basjoo 63, 134
myrtle, crape 10, 43, 74, 125, 126
Myrtus communis 33

Nandina domestica 53, 61, 130
Nelumbo nucifera 84, 133, 134
nutmeg yew 43, 53, 110, 124
Nymphaea spp. 133, 134

oak 33, 43
olive, fragrant 24, 33

Ophiopogon 29, 40, 47, 51, 53, 54, 61, 91; *O. japonicus* 33, 43, 63, 130; *O. planiscapus* 'Nigrescens' 29, 130
orange: mandarin 15, 43, 98; trifoliate 126
Osmanthus x *fortunei* 124; *O. fragrans* f. *aurantiacus* 24, 33, 100, 130; *O. heterophyllus* 29, 67, 70, 124
ostrich fern 63, 132
Ozothamnus ledifolius 136; *O. thyrosoides* 136

Pachysandra terminalis 63, 136
pagoda tree 126
Paeonia suffruticosa 130
peach, flowering 17
pepper 43, 128
persimmon 33
Phormium tenax 136
Photinia glabra 29, 40, 70, 128
Phuopsis stylosa 136
Phyllostachys bambusoides 132; *P. edulis* 132; *P. nigra* 43, 132; *P. pubescens* f. *heterocycla* 132; *P. sulphurea* 43, 132
Physalis alkekengi 43, 63, 130, 131, 134
Pieris japonica 24, 33, 43, 53, 54, 55, 73, 128
pine: bonsai 13; dry gardens 43; groupings 73; on islands 33; lower branches removed 57; by ponds 20, 29; pruning 53, 69, 72; tea gardens 51; trained 60; by waterfall 89
pines: black 72, 124; red 72, 124; umbrella 33, 66, 124; white 33, 38, 69, 72, 124; yew 33, 67, 70
Pinus densiflora 72, 124; *P. parviflora* 33, 43, 72, 124; *P. thunbergii* 43, 72, 124
plantain lily 10, 134
Platycodon grandiflorum 33, 43, 53, 63, 108, 134
Pleioblastus auricoma 132; *P. simonii* 132; *P. variegatus* 132
Podocarpus macrophyllus 33, 67, 68, 70, 124
Pogonatum contortum 132; *P. grandifolium* 132
Polygonatum falcatum 53, 134
Polystichum polyblepharum 132
Polytrichum commune 132
Poncirus trifoliata 126
Primula elatior 124
privet 43, 70
Prunus hillieri 'Spire' 13; *P. incisa* 128; *P. jamasakura* 128; *P. mume* 33, 40, 43, 51, 128; *P. Sato-zakura* 128; *P. subhirtella* 128; *P. x yedoensis* 128

Quercus dentata 43; *Q. myrsinifolia* 124

red pine 72, 124
Reeves's spiraea 33, 130
Reineckea carnea 33, 63, 130
Rhaphiolepis umbellata 53, 130
Rohdea japonica 63, 134
rhododendron 10
Rhododendron japonicum 43, 66, 130; *R. quinquefolium* 10, 43, 53, 66, 123, 130; *R. reticulatum* 10, 33, 43, 66, 123, 130
Rodgersia podophylla 84
rowan 53, 126
Ruscus aculeatus 136
rush 10, 33, 53, 84, 134

Sagina 129; *S. subulata* 132
sago palm 63
Salix alba 136; *S. babylonica* 128; *S. caprea* 136; *S. gracilistyla* 128
Sarcandra glabra 130
Sarcococca confusa 136
Sasa spp. 63; *S. tsuboïana* 132; *S. veitchii* 29, 33, 132
satsuki azalea 73, 130
sawara cypress 66, 124
Saxifraga stolonifera 43, 53, 63, 127, 130
Sciadopitys verticillata 33, 66, 124

scouring rush 33, 53
sea thrift 107
Selaginella japonica 132; *S. kraussiana* 29, 132; *S. tamariscina* 33, 63, 132
Semiarundinaria kagamiana 132; *S. yashadake* 132
sequoias 20
Shibataea kumasasa 33, 43, 132
silk tree 33
Sinobambusa tootsik 68, 132
Skimmia japonica 135, 136
snake's beard 130
snowball 130
snowbell 128
snowflower 128
Solomon's seal, fragrant 53, 134
Sophora japonica 126
Sorbus commixta 53, 126
Spanish dagger 136, 137
spicebush 114
Spiraea cantoniensis 33, 130; *S. thunbergii* 33, 130
spindle 125, 126
spurge 63
Stauntonia hexaphylla 59
Steroden plumaeformis 132
Stewartia monadelpha 66, 128; *S. pseudocamellia* 10, 35, 43, 66, 74, 123, 128
Styrax japonicum 53, 123, 128
sweet rush 84
Syringa vulgaris 135, 136

Taxus cuspidata 20, 68, 110, 124; *T.* var. *nana* 33, 40, 43, 67, 70, 124
Ternstroemia gymnanthera 33, 53, 67, 69, 70, 73, 110, 124
Thujopsis dolabrata 70, 124
thyme 40; creeping 136
Thymus serpyllum 136
toad lily 33, 43, 53, 63, 123, 134
Torreya nucifera 43, 53, 110, 124
tree peony 15, 17, 40, 130
Tricyrtis hirta 33, 43, 53, 63, 134
trifoliate orange 126
Trillium grandiflorum 136, 137; *T. kamtschaticum* 136
trout-lily 33
Tsuga sieboldii 33

umbrella pine 33, 66, 124

valerian, yellow 21
Viburnum grandiflorum 136; *V. japonicum* 110, 130; *V. plicatum* f. *plicatum* 130

water-lily 84, 133
water plantain 120
Welsh poppy 136
willow 21, 26, 33, 89, 128, 136
winterberry 33, 110, 128
wisteria 47, 74, 89, 112–13
Wisteria chinensis 112; *W. floribunda* 112
witch hazel 52–3, 57, 66, 74, 126

yellow flag 84, 136, 137
yew 67, 110; dwarf 33, 40, 43, 67, 70; nutmeg 43, 53, 110, 124
yew pine 33, 67, 70
Yucca gloriosa 136, 137

Zanthoxylum piperitum 43, 128
Zelkova serrata 126
Ziziphus jujuba 94
Zoysia japonica 86